Working For Your Dreams

THE COMPLETE
Guide to

Lead Generation

MARKETING

Digital Marketing

Opt-in Email

SEO   CRM

Search Ads

Social Media

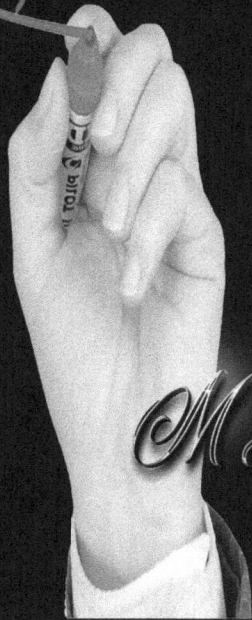

M L Ruscsak

Onboarding

Trient Press
3375 S Rainbow Blvd
#81710, SMB 13135
Las Vegas,NV 89180

Ordering Information:
Quantity sales. Special discounts are available on quantity purchases by corporations, associations, and others. For details, contact the publisher at the address above.
Orders by U.S. trade bookstores and wholesalers. Please contact Trient Press: Tel: (775) 996-3844; or visit www.trientpress.com.

Printed in the United States of America

Publisher's Cataloging-in-Publication data
Ruscsak, M.L.
A title of a book :Working for Your Dreams: The Complete Guide to Affiliate Marketing
ISBN
Paperback   978-1-955198-98-1
E-book   978-1-955198-99-8

CHAPTER 1 ONLINE VIRAL MARKETING: THE SECRET TO SUCCESS

Viral marketing is a highly sought-after approach, but it's not always easy to achieve. The reason why many people fail at it is because they don't understand what it's all about.

The key to successful viral marketing is to tap into niche networks where your target audience is already congregating online. This could be on Twitter, Facebook, or any other social media platform. People who are interested in your product or service have already formed a community online, and you can leverage this by sharing content that resonates with them.

Here's the secret: you don't have to create new content from scratch. Instead, focus on content that's already popular and widely shared within your target audience. By resharing content on different social media platforms, you increase its visibility and the chances of it going viral.

Most social media platforms have tagging and visibility boosting systems in place to help you promote your content. Utilize these systems to your advantage and drive traffic back to your website or conversion page.

To convert this traffic into sales, you can try running an ad campaign. Another effective way is to convert them into mailing list members. By building a loyal following on your mailing list, you create a recurring source of income.

By following these tips, you can save time, money, and avoid stress while increasing your chances of success with viral marketing. This guide will reveal the secrets of viral marketing that will help you achieve your marketing goals.

Don't be a Statistic: Avoid Viral Content Failure

Viral marketing relies heavily on the quality of the content you create. You want your content to spread far and wide, drawing in significant amounts of traffic that you can then convert into profit. However, creating truly viral content is not as simple as it sounds.

Many marketers fall into the trap of thinking that if they create great content, it will automatically become viral. Unfortunately, this is not the case. Simply publishing high-quality content on your blog or website is not enough to make it go viral.

Creating original, high-quality content comes at a cost, whether it be in the form of money for hiring someone to write it or the time you invest in writing it yourself. And even after investing all that resources, there is still no guarantee that your content will go viral.

To avoid joining the army of viral content failures, it's important to understand that simply publishing great content is not enough. You need a strategy for getting your content seen by the right people and making it spread. By developing a plan and leveraging the tools available to you, you can increase your chances of creating truly viral content that delivers results for your business.

Viral Success All Boils Down to the Right Eyeballs

In other words, you need to get niche viewers. The secret to viral marketing is not massive amounts of views. It is neither a tremendously mind-boggling amount of traffic. Believe it or not, raw views or raw visibility is not going to translate to much money. Seriously.

Millions of views won't produce real cash, unless those views are from the right eyeballs. Unless you're just trying to make money off YouTube videos and you get paid per thousand views, traffic, in and of itself, is not going to put food on the table.

Viral Content Pieces are Not Commodities

One of the biggest misconceptions in viral marketing is that any piece of content can be a commodity, easily transferable from one platform to another. Unfortunately, this is far from the truth. Each social media platform has its own unique audience and preferences, meaning what works on one platform may not work on another.

Take video content as an example. While videos can be incredibly effective in gaining traction on platforms like Twitter and YouTube, they may not be as well received on platforms like Pinterest or Instagram, where pictures reign supreme. Simply sharing a video on these platforms will not necessarily guarantee the same level of engagement or success.

The same can be said for text-based content, which may perform well on Twitter but not on Facebook, where images and videos tend to garner more attention.

It's important to keep in mind that content can't be treated as a commodity in viral marketing. Instead, each piece of content must be carefully crafted and tailored to suit the unique needs and preferences of each platform it's being shared on. This requires a deeper understanding of each platform's audience and a careful approach to crafting and sharing content.

In short, effective viral marketing requires a nuanced and platform-specific approach to content creation and sharing. Simply resharing content from one platform to another will not guarantee success. Instead, marketers must take the time to understand each platform and craft content that resonates with its specific audience.

The Importance of Sharing in Viral Marketing

The idea of viral marketing has long been associated with the creation of captivating and shareable content. While content is certainly a key component of a successful viral marketing campaign, there is more to it than just generating likes, comments, and favorites.

In reality, these metrics are not the end goal of a viral marketing campaign. Instead, what truly matters is the number of shares or retweets that your content receives. This is because these actions directly impact how widely your content is distributed, reaching new audiences and ultimately driving more traffic and conversions.

It's important to understand that having a piece of content that receives a lot of comments and likes is not enough. The ultimate goal is to reach the right audience, people who share the same interests as your target audience and who are likely to share your content with their own network.

The significance of sharing in viral marketing cannot be overstated. When your content is shared, it's introduced to a new audience who are likely to have similar interests, making it much easier to gain traction and reach your desired outcome.

Viral content cannot be treated as a commodity, it requires a strategic approach that takes into account the audience you want to reach and the channels that will be most effective in doing so. The majority of social signals, while they may be nice to have, are not the determining factor in the success of a viral marketing campaign.

In conclusion, while content is important, the real measure of success in viral marketing is the number of shares or retweets your content receives. By focusing on reaching the right audience and encouraging them to share your content, you can maximize your chances of success and achieve your marketing goals.

CHAPTER 2: UNDERSTANDING THE POWER OF VIRAL CONTENT

Have you ever stopped to wonder why some pieces of content seem to spread like wildfire on social media, while others barely get noticed? The truth is, viral content is everywhere, and there are many reasons why it gains traction. In this chapter, we will explore the different factors that contribute to the virality of content, from emotional appeals to shock factor and the appeal of newness. By the end of this chapter, you will have a better understanding of the elements that make content truly viral, and how you can tap into these factors to create your own viral content.

Shocking Fact: Viral Content is Everywhere!

Have you ever wondered why certain pieces of content go viral on social media? Why do people keep sharing videos, images, and posts on Facebook, Twitter, and other platforms? Well, the truth is, there is no single answer to this question, but there are several reasons why content goes viral. In this chapter, we will dive into the different factors that contribute to the virality of content on the internet.

One of the most important factors that contribute to the virality of content is its emotional appeal. When people see something that triggers an emotional response in them, whether it's humor, shock, anger, or any other emotion, they are more likely to share it with their friends and followers. This is because the content evokes a strong emotional response that people want to share with others.

Another factor that makes content go viral is its cuteness factor. Videos and images of cute animals, infants, and older people doing interesting things can often generate a lot of buzz on social media. This is because people have an innate love for all things cute and adorable, and they want to share these moments with others.

The shock factor is another common reason why content goes viral. People are often intrigued by things that are shocking, scandalous, disgraceful, or shameful. They want to know what's going on, even if they know they shouldn't be watching. It's like the appeal of a train wreck - you know you shouldn't look, but you can't help yourself.

Newness can also play a big role in making content go viral. If there's a new scientific discovery that blows people's minds, or a new piece of information that is completely unexpected, it has a high chance of going viral. People are always looking for something new and fresh, and they want to share it with others.

Finally, content can go viral if it provides new information or insights that people didn't know before. Even if they are familiar with the content, if it is presented in an interesting and engaging way, people are more likely to share it with others. This type of content is like a treat for the brain, and people can't resist sharing it.

There are several factors that contribute to the virality of content on the internet. From emotional appeal to cuteness, shock factor, newness, and information, the reasons are diverse and varied. Whether it's a video of cute kittens or a scientific discovery, there is no specific niche preference when it comes to viral content. As long as it captures people's attention and triggers an emotional response, it has a high chance of going viral.

Psychological Bases of Content Virality

Let's get one thing clear, when you're sharing stuff with your personal network, you're putting yourself out there. You're stepping out on a limb. It can blow up in your face. If you share content that a lot of people find objectionable, you may lose credibility. Still, people share content on their Facebook timelines and Twitter feeds all the time.

Why do they do it? What do they get out of it? What are the psychological factors at play?

Well, first of all, people like to share content because they want to be perceived as "hip." They want to be seen as cool or as people who know what's up with the internet. They want to be the first to share something interesting that is quickly becoming viral on the internet. There's a tremendous emotional reward associated with being the first to share interesting material.

Another reason is just to simply enjoy and exercise one's personal influence. I don't know about you, but it makes me feel really good when I share something that I am interested in or am passionate about, and my friends share and reshare that stuff.

Basically, they validate me when I see that. They tell me, in so many ways, that my opinion is important. Every share that my content gets is a vote for my personal authority, expertise and credibility.

Finally, people share content because they simply think it is valuable or interesting. In other words, it captures their range of personal interests.

And here is the secret: if these people's networks are refined enough to the point that they basically share the same set of interests, you can bet that that content will go viral.

Basically, if you like rabbits, and I like rabbits, and I post videos of cute rabbits, chances are, you will click the "share" button once you see my status update on your timeline. Chances are, you also have friends who are interested in the same things. You probably have friends who are interested in rabbits and they will share your content, and so on and so forth.

Never underestimate how "viral" shared interests could be because this is how Facebook is organized. When you add people to your friend network, chances are, they're from the same background as you. They have the same experiences, you went to the same school, and you may

have a wide range of shared interests. It is these overlapping shared interests that help fuel virality.

So What is the REAL TRUTH About Viral Content Marketing?

The phenomenon of content going viral on the internet is a complex and multifaceted one. It is driven by a range of psychological factors, from a desire to be perceived as "cool" and in-the-know, to the validation that comes from having one's opinions and interests validated by others.

One of the key drivers of content virality is the emotional reward that comes from being the first to share something interesting and new. When we share something that quickly becomes popular, it is a validation of our personal influence and credibility. This is especially true in today's world where social media platforms like Facebook and Twitter allow us to instantly share our thoughts and interests with a large network of friends and followers.

Another key factor is the psychological need to exercise personal influence and control. By sharing content that we find interesting, we are effectively asserting our authority and expertise in a particular subject. This sense of control and validation can be especially empowering, especially when our friends and followers share our content, further amplifying our personal reach and impact.

Finally, the virality of content is also driven by shared interests and experiences. When we add people to our friend network on Facebook, for example, we tend to choose people who have similar backgrounds, experiences, and interests. These overlapping interests can fuel the virality of content, as we are more likely to share and engage with content that aligns with our own interests and passions.

In conclusion, the psychological factors that drive content virality are complex and multi-faceted. From the emotional reward of being first to share something interesting, to the sense of validation and control that comes from having our opinions validated by others, to the fuel that shared interests and experiences provide, there are a range of psychological drivers that contribute to the phenomenon of content going viral.

Save Time and Money by Deciding NOT to Do This

It's important to understand that creating viral content is not a guarantee. It's a hit or miss kind of game, and the odds are not in your favor. So, instead of wasting time and money trying to create something that might not even work, why not focus on something that is proven to be effective?

One of the best ways to save time and money is to decide NOT to pursue the creation of viral content. Instead, focus on creating high-quality content that provides value to your target audience. This content will not necessarily go viral, but it will still drive traffic and convert visitors into customers.

It's also important to understand that viral content is not the only type of content that can be successful. In fact, some of the most successful content marketing campaigns are not viral at all. They're just great content that provides value to the target audience.

So, if you're trying to save time and money, don't get caught up in the idea that you need to create viral content. Instead, focus on creating high-quality content that provides value to your target audience. This is the surest way to get the results you're looking for.

In conclusion, instead of wasting time and money trying to create something that may or may not go viral, focus on creating high-quality content that provides value to your target audience. This is the most effective way to drive traffic, convert visitors into customers, and save time and money in the process.

My advice to you: don't do it. Seriously. Don't even try.

Let's get real here. Just because you think a content idea is hot and "will go viral," it won't necessarily mean that it will... In fact, in most cases, that never happens.

Unless you can read the minds of your target audience members, you would be better off not coming up with your own stuff. Coming up with some new viral content can be expensive both in terms of time and money.

Furthermore, the pursuit of viral content is a highly competitive and crowded space. The odds are stacked against you and it can take a lot of time, effort, and resources to stand out.

Instead of trying to create the next big viral sensation, consider focusing on creating high-quality, valuable content that will attract and retain your target audience. The goal of content marketing should be to build a loyal following, not just to chase after short-lived viral fame.

Here are a few tips to help you create valuable content that will attract and retain your target audience:

Know your target audience: Understanding your target audience is key to creating content that they will value and want to share. Do your research and get to know your audience's interests, pain points, and what they are looking for in a brand.

Create content that solves a problem or addresses a need: People are more likely to share content that offers a solution to a problem or addresses a need. Make sure that your content is valuable and provides real value to your target audience.

Utilize data-driven insights: Data can be a powerful tool in creating content that resonates with your target audience. Use data insights to understand what kind of content is popular, what resonates with your audience, and what drives engagement.

Be consistent: Consistency is key when it comes to building a loyal following. Make sure that you are consistently delivering high-quality content that your target audience values.

Experiment and adapt: Don't be afraid to try new things and experiment with different content formats. Listen to your audience and adjust your approach based on the feedback you receive.

In conclusion, chasing after viral content can be a time-consuming and expensive endeavor with no guaranteed outcome. Instead, focus on creating valuable content that addresses the needs of your target audience and provides real value. This will help you build a loyal following, which is the key to long-term success in content marketing.

The Better Way

So, what's the better way of doing viral content marketing? By finding proven winners in your niche and piggybacking on them.

Here's a step-by-step approach to make the most of your viral content marketing efforts:

Identify your niche: Zero in on the specific market that you want to target. Not all viral content will be relevant to your niche, so it's important to focus on content that is specific to your target audience.

Look for proven winners: Analyze the number of shares and retweets a piece of content has received. This is a good indicator of how viral it is.

Add a call to action: Once you have found a piece of viral content that is relevant to your niche, add a call to action that filters your target audience. This will ensure that only people who are interested in your niche will click through.

Focus on what counts: Don't waste time on social engagement signals that don't drive results. Focus on the number of times a piece of content has been shared or retweeted.

Pre-qualify your audience: By adding a call to action to a piece of viral content, you are pre-qualifying your audience and ensuring that only people who are interested in your niche will click through.

By following this approach, you can save time and money by piggybacking on proven viral content in your niche and reaching a highly-qualified audience with a call to action. This is the better way of doing viral content marketing and will ultimately lead to better results.

The Two-Step Trick to Effective Viral Marketing

Hey there! If you want to make your viral marketing campaigns truly effective, you've come to the right place. The steps I'm going to share with you will help you make the most of your social media, blog, forum postings, and other online marketing efforts.

Step #1: Find What's Trending

The first step is to find what's trending on the internet. With so many pictures, links, picture quotes, and videos going viral all the time, it's important to find the ones that are relevant to your target audience. For example, if you're promoting a plumbing service company in Central Florida, it might be tempting to share funny dog videos riding scooters, but that might not necessarily book you new appointments with clients. You want to find content that is closely related to your target niche.

Step #2: Share Viral Content to Drive Conversions

It's crucial to understand why you're doing viral marketing in the first place. A lot of people focus on getting as many clicks as possible, but that's not the point. The point is to drive conversions. You want to get the right people to your website so they can take an action that increases your revenue.

It's not about the traffic, it's about the conversions. It's better to have 1,000 highly targeted visitors than 1 million random visitors who might not convert into paying customers. So, your goal should be to share viral content that drives conversions.

Share the content on your blog and reshare the link on social media to drive traffic to your blog. From there, convert the traffic into potential sales by getting visitors to sign up for your newsletter. This way, you can send them updates and either upsell them to affiliate products or sell your own products. The possibilities are endless.

Your email list is the key to converting these visitors into paying customers. By sending high-quality updates, you can turn the traffic into potential sales. This is why your viral marketing campaign should focus on driving conversions to your newsletter. The more people you have on your newsletter and the higher the quality of your updates, the more money you stand to make in the long run.

PART 2 EMAIL MARKETING HACK & TIPS

CHAPTER 3: INTRODUCTION TO 21 EMAIL MARKETING HACKS

Welcome to Chapter 3! In this chapter, we will dive into the world of email marketing and its importance in today's digital marketing landscape. Before we jump into the 21 email marketing hacks, let's quickly recap what we covered in the previous chapter.

Chapter 2 discussed the Two-Step Trick to Effective Viral Marketing. We talked about the importance of finding hot and relevant content related to your niche and sharing it to drive conversions. We also touched upon the importance of getting the right kind of traffic to your site and focusing on driving conversions rather than just increasing the number of clicks to your website.

Now, let's move on to email marketing and its significance in a comprehensive digital marketing strategy. In today's world, where the internet is crowded with billions of websites and social media accounts, it's essential to have a solid email marketing plan in place. Email marketing is a powerful tool that can help you reach out to your target audience, drive conversions, and grow your business.

In this chapter, we will explore 21 email marketing hacks that you can use to improve your email marketing efforts. These hacks range from simple tips to increase open rates to more advanced strategies to maximize conversions. Whether you're a seasoned email marketer or just starting out, this chapter has something for everyone. So, let's get started!

CHAPTER 4 EMAIL MARKETING HACK #1: SEGMENT YOUR EMAIL LIST

Explanation of email list segmentation
Benefits of segmenting email list
How to segment your email lis

In Chapter 4, we'll dive into the first of our 21 email marketing hacks. This hack focuses on the importance of segmenting your email list. By dividing your email subscribers into smaller, more targeted groups, you can tailor your messages to each individual's specific interests and needs. By sending relevant, targeted messages, you'll not only increase the likelihood of your emails being read, but you'll also see a higher conversion rate. So, buckle up and let's get started with email marketing hack #1: Segment Your Email List.

Explanation of email list segmentation

What is email list segmentation?

Email list segmentation is the process of dividing your email list into smaller, more specific groups based on shared characteristics or behaviors. By doing this, you can create more targeted, personalized email campaigns that will resonate with each group.

Why is email list segmentation important?

Email list segmentation is important because it helps you to send more relevant and valuable content to your subscribers. By sending targeted and personalized emails, you increase the chances of your subscribers engaging with your content, taking action, and ultimately making a purchase.

Additionally, email list segmentation can help you to increase your open rates, click-through rates, and ultimately your conversions. This is because your subscribers are more likely to open and engage with an email that is relevant to them, rather than one that feels generic and impersonal.

How to segment your email list?

There are many ways to segment your email list, but here are some common methods:

Demographic Segmentation: This involves dividing your email list based on demographic information such as age, location, gender, and income.

Behavioral Segmentation: This involves dividing your email list based on subscriber behavior, such as how often they open your emails, what type of content they engage with, and what products they have purchased in the past.

Interest Segmentation: This involves dividing your email list based on the interests and hobbies of your subscribers. For example, you could segment your email list based on interests such as sports, cooking, or travel.

Purchasing behavior Segmentation: This involves dividing your email list based on past purchasing behavior, such as the products they have purchased, the frequency of their purchases, and their lifetime customer value.

Email list segmentation is a powerful email marketing tool that can help you to increase your open rates, click-through rates, and ultimately your conversions. By sending targeted and personalized emails, you can build a stronger relationship with your subscribers and drive more sales for your business. So, if you haven't started segmenting your email list yet, now is the time to start!

Benefits of segmenting email list

In the previous chapter, we discussed the first email marketing hack: segmenting your email list. In this chapter, we will delve deeper into why this hack is so important and what benefits it can bring to your business.

First and foremost, segmenting your email list allows you to deliver personalized, targeted messages to your subscribers. Instead of sending out a generic email to your entire list, you can divide your list into smaller groups based on specific criteria such as demographics, behavior, and interests. This enables you to tailor your messaging to the specific needs and wants of each segment, leading to higher engagement and increased conversions.

Additionally, segmenting your email list can help you improve your deliverability rates. By sending targeted, relevant messages to each segment, you are less likely to end up in the recipient's spam folder. This means that your subscribers are more likely to see your messages, which in turn can lead to higher open and click-through rates.

Another benefit of segmenting your email list is that it enables you to track and analyze your email marketing efforts more effectively. By measuring the success of your email campaigns on a segment-by-segment basis, you can gain valuable insights into what is working and what isn't. This information can then be used to optimize your future email campaigns, making them even more effective.

Segmenting your email list also allows you to test and refine your email marketing strategy. By experimenting with different messaging, subject lines, and calls-to-action for each segment, you can find what resonates with each group and then use this information to optimize your overall email marketing strategy.

Finally, segmenting your email list can lead to increased customer loyalty and engagement. When your subscribers receive messages that are relevant, personalized, and targeted specifically to their interests and needs, they are more likely to engage with your brand. This can lead to increased brand awareness, customer loyalty, and repeat business, all of which are crucial for the long-term success of your business.

Segmenting your email list is a powerful email marketing hack that can bring numerous benefits to your business. From increased personalization and relevance to improved deliverability and enhanced insights, there are many reasons to segment your email list and reap the rewards of a more effective email marketing strategy.

How to segment your email list

Segmenting your email list is a critical step in any email marketing campaign. By dividing your email list into smaller, more specific groups, you can tailor your messaging to each group, making your emails more targeted and relevant to each recipient. This leads to higher engagement rates, increased conversions, and ultimately, better results from your email marketing efforts.

So, how exactly do you go about segmenting your email list? Here are some steps to help you get started:

Determine your audience segments: Before you start dividing your email list into segments, you need to determine which segments you want to create. Consider factors like demographics, location, interests, buying behavior, and more to determine the best way to divide your list.

Gather information on your subscribers: Once you know the segments you want to create, you need to gather information on your subscribers. This could include information like their age, location, interests, purchase history, and more. You can gather this information through forms on your website, surveys, and other methods.

Use email marketing software: Email marketing software, like Mailchimp or Constant Contact, makes it easy to segment your email list. Most of these tools come with built-in segmentation options, allowing you to quickly and easily divide your list into specific groups.

Create segments based on subscriber behavior: One of the most effective ways to segment your email list is based on subscriber behavior. For example, you can create segments for subscribers who have opened a certain number of emails, clicked on specific links, made a purchase, and more.

Personalize your messaging: Once you have your email list segments created, it's time to start personalizing your messaging. Use the information you gathered on your subscribers to craft emails that are tailored to each specific group. This could include customizing the subject line, content, and even the call to action based on the segment you are targeting.

By following these steps, you can effectively segment your email list, making your email marketing campaigns more effective and engaging. Remember, the more you personalize your messaging and make your emails relevant to each recipient, the more likely they are to engage with your emails, leading to better results from your email marketing efforts.

CHAPTER 5 EMAIL MARKETING HACK #2: PERSONALIZE YOUR EMAILS

Explanation of personalized emails
Benefits of personalizing emails
How to personalize your emails

Personalization is a powerful tool in email marketing, allowing you to create a more intimate and personalized experience for your subscribers. By including the recipient's name, location, or other specific information, you can make the recipient feel valued and increase the chances of your email being opened and acted upon. In this chapter, we will explore the benefits of personalizing your emails and how to effectively implement it in your email marketing strategy. From using dynamic content to including personalized calls to action, we'll cover everything you need to know to take your email marketing to the next level with personalization.

Explanation of personalized emails

Personalized emails are a type of email marketing strategy where the content of the email is tailored to the specific recipient. This is achieved by incorporating the recipient's name, location, interests, past purchases, or any other relevant information into the email content. Personalized emails aim to create a more personalized experience for the recipient and increase the likelihood of engagement.

Personalized emails can take many forms, from simple greetings using the recipient's name, to highly customized content that includes product recommendations, special offers, and other information that is relevant to the recipient. The goal is to create a sense of connection and relevance with the recipient, making the email more engaging and increasing the chances of it being acted upon.

There are many benefits to using personalized emails, including higher open rates, increased click-through rates, and better conversions. Personalized emails also help to build stronger relationships with customers and increase brand loyalty. By showing that you understand your customers' needs and preferences, you can build trust and increase the likelihood of repeat business.

In short, personalized emails are an effective way to reach your target audience, build stronger relationships, and drive better results for your email marketing campaigns. By taking the time to understand your customers and tailoring your content to their specific needs and interests, you can create highly effective, personalized email campaigns that engage your audience and drive conversions.

Benefits of personalizing emails

Personalizing emails is a critical aspect of email marketing that can help businesses enhance their relationship with customers. By including personal touches in emails, businesses can make customers feel special and valued. Personalized emails are a great way to build trust and loyalty, and they can result in higher open rates, click-through rates, and conversions.

There are several benefits to personalizing emails, including:

Increased engagement: Personalized emails are more likely to be opened and read because they address the recipient by name and speak directly to their interests and needs. This increased engagement can lead to higher click-through rates and conversions.

Better targeting: Personalizing emails allows businesses to send highly targeted messages that are relevant to each recipient. This leads to a better customer experience, as recipients are more likely to be interested in the content of the email.

Increased customer loyalty: Personalizing emails can help build stronger relationships with customers by making them feel valued and appreciated. This increased sense of loyalty can lead to repeat business and positive word-of-mouth recommendations.

Improved deliverability: Personalized emails are less likely to be marked as spam because they appear more trustworthy and relevant to the recipient. This improved deliverability can lead to a higher inbox placement rate, which means more of your emails are delivered to your customers' inboxes.

Better ROI: Personalizing emails can result in higher open rates, click-through rates, and conversions. This can translate into a higher return on investment (ROI) for businesses, as they are able to achieve better results with the same amount of resources.

In conclusion, personalizing emails can provide a number of benefits for businesses. By addressing each recipient by name and providing targeted and relevant content, businesses can build stronger relationships with customers, improve their email deliverability, and achieve a higher ROI.

Example Non-Personalized E-mail

Subject: New Product Launch

Dear Customer,

We are excited to announce the launch of our new product. This innovative product has been designed to meet your needs and improve your overall experience.

Please visit our website to learn more about the features and benefits of this new product. We are confident that you will love it as much as we do.

Thank you for choosing [Company Name].

Best regards,
[Company Name]

P.   S. Don't forget to follow us on social media for the latest news and updates.

Example Personalized E-mail

Subject: Welcome to Our Community, [First Name]!

Dear [First Name],

We're thrilled to have you join our community! Our goal is to provide you with the resources and support you need to achieve your goals and make the most of your experience with us.

We noticed that you're interested in [interest], and we wanted to make sure you're aware of all the resources and opportunities we have available in that area. Whether it's through our online forums, monthly webinars, or expert-led workshops, we're confident that you'll find something that meets your needs.

If there's anything specific you're looking for or any questions you have, don't hesitate to reach out to us. Our team is here to support you, and we're always happy to help.

Best regards,

[Your Name]

[Company Name]

How to Personalize Your Emails

Personalizing your emails is a crucial aspect of email marketing that can help you stand out from the rest of the crowd and increase the chances of your email being read, clicked and acted upon. Personalizing emails not only adds a personal touch to your communication with your audience, but it also shows your recipients that you value and respect their time, which can lead to improved customer loyalty and engagement.

In this chapter, we will outline some of the key steps for personalizing your emails:

Gather information about your recipients: The more information you have about your recipients, the more personalized you can make your emails. Some of the information you can gather include their name, location, purchase history, preferences and interests.

Use dynamic content: Dynamic content is a type of content that changes based on the recipient's preferences, behavior or location. This type of personalization can help you target your audience more effectively and increase engagement.

Address your recipient by name: Including your recipient's name in the email subject line or greeting line is a simple way to make your email feel more personal and relevant.

Segment your email list: By segmenting your email list based on your recipients' preferences, you can create targeted and personalized campaigns that are more likely to resonate with your audience.

Use data to inform your email strategy: By analyzing your email data and understanding your audience, you can gain insights into their preferences and behavior, and use that information to create more personalized email campaigns.

Test and iterate: Personalizing your emails is an ongoing process, and it's important to continuously test and refine your approach to ensure that you are delivering the most effective and personalized emails possible.

By following these steps, you can effectively personalize your emails and deliver more effective campaigns that engage and resonate with your audience. Whether you are sending an email newsletter, promotional offer or just keeping in touch with your subscribers, personalizing your emails can help you establish a deeper connection with your audience and ultimately drive better results.

CHAPTER 6 EMAIL MARKETING HACK #3: OPTIMIZE YOUR EMAIL SUBJECT LINE

Explanation of optimized email subject lines
Benefits of optimized subject lines
How to optimize your email subject lines

In this chapter, we will delve into the third email marketing hack, which is optimizing your email subject line. The subject line is the first thing your recipient sees, and it can make or break your email's success. The subject line determines whether your recipient will open the email or mark it as spam. Hence, it is crucial to optimize your subject line to grab the recipient's attention and entice them to open your email.

Explanation of Optimized Email Subject Line:
An optimized email subject line is one that is well-crafted, compelling, and relevant to the recipient. It should be short, concise, and to the point, while also accurately reflecting the content of the email. The subject line should also be optimized for readability, meaning that it should be free of typos, grammar errors, and all-caps text.

Benefits of Optimizing Your Email Subject Line:

Increased Open Rates: A well-crafted subject line can increase the open rates of your emails, which means that more people are reading your messages.

Improved Engagement: A subject line that accurately reflects the content of the email and entices the recipient to open the message will lead to improved engagement.

Better Deliverability: A subject line that is optimized for readability and relevance will be more likely to avoid spam filters and land in the recipient's inbox.

Better Branding: An optimized subject line can help to establish your brand and make your emails more recognizable.

How to Optimize Your Email Subject Line:

Keep it Short: The subject line should be short and concise, preferably less than 50 characters.

Be Descriptive: The subject line should accurately reflect the content of the email and give the recipient a clear idea of what to expect.

Use Action-Oriented Language: Use language that is active, and encourage the recipient to take action.

Personalize the Subject Line: Use the recipient's name or other personal information to make the subject line more personalized.

Test, Test, Test: Test different subject lines to see what works best for your target audience.

Conclusion:
In conclusion, optimizing your email subject line is a critical aspect of email marketing that can help you increase open rates, improve engagement, and better establish your brand. By keeping it short, descriptive, and using action-oriented language, you can craft subject lines that entice your recipients to open your emails and take action.

CHAPTER 7 EMAIL MARKETING HACK #4: USE A CLEAR CALL-TO-ACTION

Explanation of call-to-action
Benefits of clear call-to-action
How to use clear call-to-action in emails

In this chapter, we will discuss one of the most important elements of a successful email marketing campaign - the call-to-action (CTA). A clear and well-placed call-to-action can greatly increase the effectiveness of your email marketing efforts and lead to higher conversion rates.

Explanation of Call-to-Action:
A call-to-action (CTA) is a crucial component of any effective email marketing campaign. Its purpose is to encourage the recipient to take a specific action, such as making a purchase, downloading a resource, filling out a form, or subscribing to a newsletter. A clear and well-crafted CTA can help drive engagement and conversion in your emails.

A call-to-action is usually represented by a button or a link, and it should be prominently displayed in your emails so that it is easy for the recipient to see and act on. A good CTA should be attention-grabbing, memorable, and actionable, with a clear and concise message that clearly communicates the next step the recipient should take.

For example, if you are promoting a new product, a CTA might be something like "Shop Now" or "Get Yours Today." If you are offering a free resource, your CTA might be "Download Now" or "Get Your Free Guide." In each case, the CTA should be directly tied to the goal of the email and should be prominently displayed so that it is easily noticeable and actionable.

It's important to note that not all emails need a CTA. For instance, if your email is purely informational or a newsletter, it may not require a CTA. However, if your goal is to drive engagement or conversion, it's important to include a clear and effective CTA in your emails.

In summary, the call-to-action is a key component of any email marketing campaign and can help drive engagement and conversion. A clear and well-crafted CTA should be attention-grabbing, memorable, and actionable, with a clear message that communicates the next step the recipient should take.

Benefits of Using a Clear Call-to-Action:

Using a clear call-to-action in your emails can have numerous benefits, including:

Increased conversion rates
Better engagement with your audience
Improved brand recognition and trust
Better tracking of email marketing success

How to Use a Clear Call-to-Action in Your Emails:

A call-to-action (CTA) is the primary means of driving engagement and conversion in your emails. It is a button or link that encourages the recipient to take a specific action, such as making a purchase, downloading a resource, or filling out a form.

To use a clear call-to-action in your emails, you should follow these steps:

Determine the desired action: The first step in using a clear call-to-action is to determine the desired action you want the recipient to take. This could be anything from making a purchase to downloading a resource or filling out a form.

Make it prominent and easy to find: Once you have determined the desired action, you need to make the call-to-action prominent and easy to find in the email. This means that it should be placed in a prominent position within the email and made to stand out visually.

Use action-oriented language: When writing the call-to-action, it's important to use action-oriented language. Use words and phrases that encourage the recipient to take action, such as "click here," "get started," or "download now."

Make it visually standout: To make the call-to-action even more prominent, consider making it stand out visually. This could be done by using a different color, font, or size, or by using an eye-catching graphic or button.

Test and optimize: Finally, test and optimize your call-to-action for maximum effectiveness. Try different variations of the text, placement, and design to see what resonates best with your audience.

By following these steps, you can create clear and effective calls-to-action in your emails that drive engagement and conversion.

Conclusion:
Incorporating a clear and well-placed call-to-action in your emails is crucial for driving engagement and conversion. By following the steps outlined above, you can effectively use CTAs to achieve your email marketing goals and improve the overall success of your campaigns.

Chapter 8 Email Marketing Hack #5: Make Your Emails Mobile-Friendly
Explanation of mobile-friendly emails
Benefits of mobile-friendly emails
How to make your emails mobile-friendly

With the increasing use of smartphones and other mobile devices, it is essential for businesses to ensure that their emails are optimized for mobile devices. In this chapter, we will explore the importance of making your emails mobile-friendly and provide tips on how to do so.

Explanation of Mobile-Friendly Emails:

In today's world, more and more people are accessing their emails on their mobile devices. This means that it is crucial for businesses to ensure that their emails are mobile-friendly, as this will improve their chances of success and engagement with their audience.

Explanation of Mobile-Friendly Emails:
A mobile-friendly email is one that can be easily read and interacted with on a mobile device. This means that the email should have a responsive design that adjusts to the size of the device screen and is easy to navigate with a finger or stylus. In addition, mobile-friendly emails should have larger text, larger buttons, and plenty of white space to make them easy to read and navigate.

Benefits of Mobile-Friendly Emails:
There are many benefits to making your emails mobile-friendly, including:

Increased engagement: By making it easy for your audience to access and interact with your emails on their mobile devices, you are more likely to keep their attention and drive engagement.
Improved deliverability: Many email providers prioritize mobile-friendly emails in their inboxes, which can improve your chances of success.
Higher conversion rates: Mobile-friendly emails are more likely to convert as they are easier to interact with and navigate, which can lead to more sales and conversions.

How to Make Your Emails Mobile-Friendly:
To make your emails mobile-friendly, you should follow these steps:

Use responsive design: Ensure that your emails adjust to the size of the device screen and are easy to navigate.

Keep text large and readable: Make sure that your text is large enough to be easily read on a mobile device.

Use larger buttons: Larger buttons are easier to tap with a finger or stylus, making it easier for your audience to interact with your email.

Include plenty of white space: This makes your emails easier to read and navigate on a mobile device.

Conclusion:

Making your emails mobile-friendly is crucial in today's world, where more and more people are accessing their emails on their mobile devices. By following the steps outlined in this chapter, you can improve your chances of success and drive engagement with your audience.

Benefits of Mobile-Friendly Emails:

There are several benefits to making your emails mobile-friendly, including:

One of the key benefits of having mobile-friendly emails is increased engagement and open rates. With more and more people accessing their emails on their mobile devices, it's important to ensure that your emails are optimized for viewing on smaller screens. A mobile-friendly email will be more likely to be opened and interacted with on mobile devices, leading to higher engagement and open rates.

Another benefit of mobile-friendly emails is improved user experience. A mobile-friendly email is designed to be easy to read and navigate on a small screen, making it a better experience for the recipient. This improved user experience can make recipients more likely to take the desired action, such as making a purchase or filling out a form.

Finally, mobile-friendly emails can lead to increased conversion rates. By providing a better user experience, mobile-friendly emails can lead to increased conversions and more sales or leads. This makes mobile-friendliness an important consideration for any email marketing campaign.

In conclusion, making your emails mobile-friendly has numerous benefits, including increased engagement and open rates, improved user experience, and increased conversion rates. To maximize the impact of your email marketing campaigns, it's important to ensure that your emails are optimized for viewing on mobile devices.

How to Make Your Emails Mobile-Friendly:

To make your emails mobile-friendly, you should follow these steps:

In order to make your emails mobile-friendly, it's important to follow a few key principles. These include using a responsive design, making text and buttons large and easy to click, providing plenty of white space, and testing your emails on different devices.

Use a responsive design: A responsive design will automatically adjust the size and layout of your email based on the size of the device screen. This means that your email will look great and be easy to navigate on any device, whether it's a smartphone or tablet.

Make text and buttons large and easy to click: Use large, legible text and buttons that are easy to click with a finger or stylus. This will make it easier for the recipient to take the desired action, such as making a purchase or downloading a resource.

Provide plenty of white space: Use plenty of white space to make the email easier to read and navigate. This will help the recipient focus on the most important information and increase the chances of them taking the desired action.

Test your emails on different devices: Test your emails on different devices, such as smartphones and tablets, to ensure that they are mobile-friendly. This will allow you to make any necessary adjustments and ensure that your emails are optimized for all devices.

By following these principles, you can ensure that your emails are mobile-friendly and provide a great user experience for your recipients, which can lead to increased engagement and conversion rates.Conclusion:

Making your emails mobile-friendly is essential in today's increasingly mobile world. By providing a better user experience and increased engagement, mobile-friendly emails can lead to higher conversion rates and more sales or leads. By following the tips outlined in this chapter, you can ensure that your emails are optimized for mobile devices and provide the best possible experience for your recipients.

CHAPTER 8 EMAIL MARKETING HACK #5: MAKE YOUR EMAILS MOBILE-FRIENDLY

Explanation of mobile-friendly emails
Benefits of mobile-friendly emails
How to make your emails mobile-friendly

Explanation of mobile-friendly emails

As more and more people access their email on their mobile devices, it's crucial to ensure that your emails are optimized for mobile viewing. A mobile-friendly email is one that can be easily read and interacted with on a mobile device, providing a better user experience for the recipient. In this chapter, we will explore the definition of mobile-friendly emails, the benefits they provide, and how you can make your emails mobile-friendly. By the end of this chapter, you will have a solid understanding of the importance of mobile-friendliness in email marketing and how you can ensure that your emails are optimized for mobile viewing.

In today's digital age, more and more people are checking their emails on their mobile devices. As a result, it's essential for businesses to ensure that their emails are optimized for mobile devices. This is where mobile-friendly emails come into play.

A mobile-friendly email is an email that can be easily read and interacted with on a mobile device. This means that the email should have a responsive design that adjusts to the size of the device screen and is easy to navigate with a finger or stylus. In addition, mobile-friendly emails should have larger text, larger buttons, and plenty of white space to make them easy to read and navigate.

Having mobile-friendly emails is crucial for businesses because it ensures that their emails are being seen and interacted with by their audience. With the majority of people checking their emails on their mobile devices, it's more important than ever to have emails that are optimized for mobile. This can lead to increased engagement, open rates, and conversion rates.

In short, mobile-friendly emails are essential for businesses looking to reach and engage their audience in today's digital world. By making sure that their emails are optimized for mobile devices, businesses can ensure that their messages are being seen and acted upon by their audience.

Benefits of mobile-friendly emails

In today's world, where a majority of the population is using mobile devices to access the internet and check their emails, it's imperative that your emails are mobile-friendly. Having mobile-friendly emails not only ensures that your recipients have a great user experience but also helps to increase the success of your email marketing campaigns.

Here are some of the key benefits of using mobile-friendly emails:

Increased engagement and open rates: A mobile-friendly email is optimized to be easily readable on smaller screens and is more likely to be opened and interacted with on mobile devices, leading to higher engagement and open rates.

Improved user experience: When your emails are mobile-friendly, your recipients have a better user experience, which can lead to higher satisfaction levels and make them more likely to take the desired action.

Increased conversion rates: By providing a better user experience, mobile-friendly emails can lead to increased conversion rates, which in turn can result in more sales or leads for your business.

Better accessibility: Mobile-friendly emails are accessible to a wider audience, including people with visual impairments or who use assistive technologies such as screen readers.

Enhanced brand image: By providing a great user experience through mobile-friendly emails, you can enhance your brand's image and reputation, which can lead to increased loyalty and long-term customer relationships.

In conclusion, making your emails mobile-friendly is crucial in today's digital landscape, and the benefits it offers are numerous. By providing a better user experience, you can increase the success of your email marketing campaigns and build stronger relationships with your customers.

How to Make Your Emails Mobile-Friendly

Making your emails mobile-friendly is essential in today's world, where more and more people are using their mobile devices to check their emails. A mobile-friendly email will provide a better user experience for your recipients and increase the chances of them taking the desired action. Here are the steps you need to take to make your emails mobile-friendly:

Use a responsive design: A responsive design will automatically adjust the size and layout of your email based on the size of the device screen. This ensures that your email will look great and be easy to navigate on any device, whether it's a smartphone, tablet, or computer.

Make text and buttons large and easy to click: Use large, legible text and buttons that are easy to click with a finger or stylus. This makes it easier for the recipient to navigate and take action on your email.

Provide plenty of white space: Use plenty of white space to make the email easier to read and navigate. This helps to break up the content and make it more visually appealing.

Test your emails on different devices: Test your emails on different devices, such as smartphones and tablets, to ensure that they are mobile-friendly. This will help you to identify any issues and make any necessary adjustments before you send the email.

By following these steps, you can ensure that your emails are mobile-friendly and provide a great user experience for your recipients. This will help to increase engagement and conversions, making your email marketing efforts even more effective.

CHAPTER 9 EMAIL MARKETING HACK #6: KEEP YOUR EMAILS SHORT AND SWEET

Explanation of short and sweet emails
Benefits of short and sweet emails
How to keep your emails short and sweet

In today's fast-paced digital world, people are constantly bombarded with emails and other forms of communication. To stand out and engage your audience, it's important to keep your emails short and sweet. By doing so, you can ensure that your emails are easily digestible and that the recipient is more likely to take the desired action.

Explanation of short and sweet emails:
Short and sweet emails are a popular choice for many businesses and organizations because they are highly effective in getting their message across to the recipient. In today's fast-paced world, people are bombarded with an endless stream of information, making it difficult to focus and retain important details. By keeping emails short and sweet, businesses and organizations can help ensure that their message is not lost in the noise and that it is more likely to be read and acted upon.

In addition, short and sweet emails are highly beneficial for both the sender and the recipient. For the sender, they save time and resources by allowing them to quickly and effectively communicate with their audience. For the recipient, they are easy to read, understand, and act upon, making the email experience more enjoyable and less overwhelming.

In summary, short and sweet emails are a valuable tool for businesses and organizations looking to effectively communicate with their audience. By keeping emails concise and focused, they can help ensure that their message is not lost in the noise and that it is more likely to be read and acted upon.

Benefits of short and sweet emails:

Short and sweet emails are a powerful tool for email marketing, offering several key benefits to marketers and businesses. Here are a few of the key advantages of keeping your emails short and sweet:

Increased Open Rates: One of the primary benefits of short and sweet emails is that they are more likely to be opened and read by the recipient. This is because they get straight to the point, providing only the most important information, and they are quick and easy to read. In addition, short and sweet emails are less likely to be marked as spam, which means that they are more likely to reach the inbox of the recipient.

Improved Engagement: By getting straight to the point, you are more likely to engage the recipient and get them to take the desired action. For example, if you are trying to sell a product, you can provide a clear and concise description of the product, its benefits, and how to purchase it. By providing all of this information in a clear and concise manner, you are more likely to get the recipient to take the desired action.

Higher Conversion Rates: By providing a clear and concise message, short and sweet emails can lead to higher conversion rates. This is because the recipient is more likely to understand the message, and they are more likely to take the desired action if the message is clear and easy to understand. In addition, short and sweet emails are less likely to be discarded or ignored, which means that they are more likely to result in a conversion.

Overall, the benefits of short and sweet emails are clear, and they provide a powerful tool for email marketing. By keeping your emails concise and to-the-point, you can increase open rates, improve engagement, and drive higher conversion rates.

How to keep your emails short and sweet:

Email marketing is a powerful tool, but only if your messages are read and acted upon. One way to increase the chances of this happening is to keep your emails short and sweet. Here are some tips on how to do just that:

Focus on one main message: Make sure that each email has a clear, focused message. Avoid adding any extra information that is not essential to the purpose of the email.

Use short paragraphs and bullet points: Break up your text into short paragraphs and use bullet points to make it easier to read. This makes the email more visually appealing and easier to scan for information.

Get to the point quickly: Start your email with the most important information and avoid any unnecessary introductions. The recipient should be able to tell what the email is about from the first few lines.

Avoid clutter: Keep your emails free from clutter and avoid using any distracting graphics or images. A clean and simple design can help the recipient focus on the message and take the desired action.

By following these tips, you can ensure that your emails are short, sweet, and effective. Your audience will appreciate the quick and easy-to-read format, and you will see improved engagement and higher conversion rates as a result.

 Here's an example of a wrong email versus a short and sweet one:

Wrong email:

Subject: Greetings from ABC Company

Dear [Name],

I hope this email finds you well. My name is [Your Name], and I am writing to you today from ABC Company, a leading provider of [products/services]. I would like to take this opportunity to introduce our company and the fantastic products/services that we offer.

At ABC Company, we are committed to providing our customers with the best quality products and services. Our goal is to ensure that our customers are completely satisfied with our products/services and that they receive the best possible value for their money.

We would be delighted if you would take a few moments to visit our website and see the products/services we have to offer. If you have any questions, please don't hesitate to contact us.

Thank you for taking the time to read this email. We look forward to the opportunity to work with you in the future.

Best regards,
[Your Name]

Short and sweet email:

Subject: [Your main message]

[Name],

[Your main message in a few sentences].

Visit [Website/link to learn more].

Best regards,
[Your Name]

CHAPTER 10 EMAIL MARKETING HACK #7: TEST, TEST, TEST

Explanation of testing
Benefits of testing
How to test your emails

Email marketing is a constantly evolving field, and it's essential to stay ahead of the curve by constantly testing and refining your approach. In this chapter, we'll explore the importance of testing in email marketing and how it can help you achieve better results. We'll also look at the benefits of testing and how you can go about testing your emails to ensure they're performing at their best. Whether you're a seasoned email marketer or just starting out, this chapter will provide you with the knowledge and tips you need to improve your email campaigns and drive more conversions. So, let's dive in and discover the power of testing in email marketing!

Explanation of testing

Testing is an essential part of email marketing. It involves sending your emails to a small group of recipients before sending it to your entire email list. The purpose of testing is to identify any issues or problems with the email, such as formatting errors, broken links, or incorrect images. By testing your emails, you can ensure that they are working as intended and that they provide a positive experience for your recipients.

Testing can also be used to compare different versions of the same email to see which one performs better. This type of testing is known as A/B testing and involves sending two versions of the same email to two different groups of recipients. The results of the test can then be used to determine which version is more effective and make improvements to future emails.

Overall, testing is an important part of email marketing as it helps you to improve the quality and effectiveness of your emails, and ensures that your recipients have a positive experience when they receive your emails.

Benefits of testing

Testing is a critical component of any successful email marketing campaign. By testing different elements of your emails, you can identify what works best and make improvements that will help increase engagement and conversion rates. The benefits of testing include:

Improved open rates: By testing different subject lines and sending times, you can identify the elements that lead to higher open rates.

Increased engagement: Testing different content, calls-to-action, and design elements can help you find what resonates with your audience and increase engagement.

Higher conversion rates: By testing different elements of your emails, you can identify what drives conversions and make improvements that will result in higher conversion rates.

Increased ROI: By testing and improving your emails, you can increase your return on investment by making sure that your campaigns are as effective as possible.

By testing different elements of your emails, you can ensure that you are getting the best results possible from your email marketing efforts. By making data-driven decisions, you can improve the performance of your campaigns and see higher engagement, conversion rates, and return on investment.

How to test your emails

Testing is a critical aspect of email marketing and can help ensure that your emails are effective and achieving your desired results. By testing different elements of your emails, you can determine what works best for your target audience and make necessary adjustments to improve your email marketing campaigns.

Here are some key elements to test in your emails:

Subject line: Test different subject lines to determine which one leads to the highest open rate.

Email content: Test the content of your emails, including the format, tone, and language, to see what resonates best with your audience.

Call-to-action: Test the placement and design of your call-to-action buttons to see what drives the most conversions.

Images: Test the use of images and graphics to see what impact they have on your email's effectiveness.

Segmentation: Test different segments of your email list to see which segment responds best to certain messages and offers.

It's important to remember that testing should be an ongoing process, not a one-time event. Regularly testing and making adjustments to your emails will help you continuously improve your email marketing campaigns and achieve better results.

When testing, it's important to use a small sample of your email list first to avoid any negative impact on your overall results. After analyzing the results of your tests, you can then make changes and test again to see if your modifications have had the desired effect.

In conclusion, testing is a crucial step in the email marketing process that can lead to improved engagement, higher conversion rates, and better overall results. By regularly testing your emails, you can ensure that your email marketing campaigns are always performing at their best.

CHAPTER 11 EMAIL MARKETING HACK #8: USE A CONSISTENT EMAIL DESIGN

Explanation of consistent email design
Benefits of consistent email design
How to use consistent email design

Email design is a critical aspect of your email marketing strategy. The way your emails look and feel can have a significant impact on how they are received by your audience. To ensure that your emails are effective and well-received, it is important to use a consistent email design.

In this chapter, we will explore the importance of a consistent email design, the benefits it brings to your email marketing efforts, and how you can achieve it. Whether you're just starting out with email marketing or looking to improve your existing strategy, the tips and insights shared in this chapter will help you create visually appealing and effective emails that engage your audience and drive results.

Explanation of consistent email design

Consistent email design refers to the use of a uniform look and feel for all of your email communications. This includes the use of a similar color scheme, font style and size, logo placement, and other design elements. By using a consistent design, you can create a recognizable brand image and establish trust with your audience.

For example, imagine that you receive two emails from a company. The first email has a professional design with a consistent color scheme, logo placement, and font style. The second email looks completely different and has a random assortment of colors, fonts, and design elements. Which email would you be more likely to trust and engage with?

The first email, with a consistent design, is likely to create a better impression and establish trust with the recipient. This is the power of consistent email design. By using a consistent design, you can create a professional and recognizable image that will help you stand out in the inbox and improve engagement with your audience.

Benefits of consistent email design

Consistent email design has numerous benefits that can enhance your overall email marketing strategy. Some of the key benefits of consistent email design include:

Improved brand recognition: By using a consistent design, you can establish a strong brand identity and improve recognition among your target audience. Your emails will have a professional and cohesive look, which will make them easier to recognize and remember.

Increased credibility: Consistent email design can also increase the credibility of your brand. A professional and well-designed email will give your audience the impression that your company is serious about its brand and is committed to delivering high-quality content.

Enhanced user experience: Consistent email design can provide a better user experience for the recipient. A well-designed email that is easy to navigate and read will be more enjoyable for the recipient and will make them more likely to take the desired action.

Increased engagement: By providing a better user experience, consistent email design can lead to increased engagement and higher open rates. A well-designed email is more likely to be opened and interacted with by the recipient, which can lead to higher engagement and more conversions.

Improved tracking and analytics: Consistent email design can also make it easier to track and analyze the success of your email campaigns. By using a consistent design, you will be able to compare the results of different campaigns and determine which design elements are working best. This information can then be used to optimize future campaigns for even better results.

Overall, consistent email design can greatly enhance your email marketing strategy by improving brand recognition, increasing credibility, enhancing user experience, increasing engagement, and making it easier to track and analyze your campaigns.

How to use consistent email design

When it comes to email marketing, having a consistent email design can make a big impact on the success of your campaigns. A consistent design helps to build brand recognition and establish a professional image, while also making your emails easier to read and navigate. Here are some tips on how to use consistent email design in your email marketing efforts:

Establish brand guidelines: Start by defining the look and feel of your brand and establishing guidelines for your email design. This could include things like color palette, font choices, and the overall layout of your emails.

Use a template: Using a template can help to ensure that your emails maintain a consistent look and feel from one campaign to the next. Choose a template that is easy to use and customize, and make sure it aligns with your brand guidelines.

Use consistent headers and footers: Including a header and footer in your emails can help to establish brand recognition and make your emails easier to navigate. Make sure that your header and footer are consistent from one email to the next, and that they include important information like your logo and contact information.

Consistent use of images and graphics: If you decide to include images or graphics in your emails, make sure that they are consistent with your brand guidelines and the overall look and feel of your emails.

Test your design: Before sending out your emails, be sure to test your design to make sure that it looks good on different devices and email clients. You can use an email preview tool to get a sneak peek of what your emails will look like before you send them.

By following these tips, you can create a consistent email design that will help to build brand recognition and establish a professional image. Your emails will also be easier to read and navigate, which can help to improve engagement and drive better results from your email marketing campaigns.

CHAPTER 12 EMAIL MARKETING HACK #9: AUTOMATE YOUR EMAILS

Explanation of automated emails
Benefits of automated emails
How to automate your emails

Email marketing is a crucial part of any marketing strategy, and automation can help you make the most of this important channel. Automated emails are pre-written emails that are triggered by specific events, such as a subscriber signing up for your newsletter or making a purchase. By automating your emails, you can save time and improve the effectiveness of your marketing efforts.

In this chapter, we will explore the explanation of automated emails, the benefits of using them, and how you can set up automated emails for your own marketing campaigns. Whether you are new to email marketing or are a seasoned professional, this chapter will provide you with valuable insights into the power of automated emails and how you can use them to drive your business forward.

Explanation of automated emails

Automated emails are pre-written emails that are triggered by a specific action or event. Unlike manual emails, which require manual intervention, automated emails are sent automatically, providing a more efficient and effective way of reaching out to your customers. They are a crucial aspect of any successful email marketing campaign and are becoming increasingly popular among marketers.

There are several types of automated emails, including welcome emails, abandoned cart emails, and post-purchase follow-up emails. They can be used to introduce new products, offer promotions, send reminders, and provide helpful information to your subscribers. The beauty of automated emails is that they can be customized and tailored to fit the needs of your business, making it easier to engage with your customers and increase the chances of conversion.

With automated emails, you can save time, improve the efficiency of your email marketing campaigns, and provide your customers with a more personalized and relevant experience. Whether you are a small business owner or a large corporation, automated emails can help you take your email marketing to the next level.

Benefits of automated emails

Email automation has revolutionized the way businesses communicate with their customers and prospects. Automated emails are pre-written emails that are triggered to be sent based on specific actions or events. They allow businesses to save time, increase efficiency, and provide a personalized experience for their customers.

Here are some of the key benefits of using automated emails:

Increased Efficiency: Automated emails take care of the repetitive and time-consuming tasks of email marketing, freeing up valuable time for other important tasks.

Improved Personalization: Automated emails can be tailored to the specific needs and interests of each individual recipient, providing a personalized experience.

Increased Engagement: Automated emails can be set up to send at the right time, ensuring that the recipient is more likely to open and engage with the email.

Better Conversion Rates: Automated emails have been shown to have higher conversion rates compared to manual emails.

Increased Customer Satisfaction: Automated emails provide a more convenient and streamlined experience for the customer, leading to increased satisfaction and loyalty.

In short, automated emails offer a range of benefits that can help businesses achieve their email marketing goals, from increasing efficiency to improving customer satisfaction. By taking advantage of the power of automation, businesses can streamline their email marketing processes and achieve better results.

How to automate your emails

Automating your email campaigns is an effective way to reach your target audience with consistent, personalized, and timely messages. With email automation, you can set up a series of pre-written emails that are triggered by specific actions or events, such as a subscriber joining your mailing list or a customer abandoning their shopping cart. Automated emails allow you to streamline your email marketing efforts, saving you time and ensuring that your messages reach your audience at the right time and with the right content.

Here's how you can automate your emails:

Define your goals: Determine what you want to achieve with your automated email campaign, whether it's to increase engagement, boost sales, or build brand awareness.

Choose your automation platform: There are several email automation platforms available, such as Mailchimp, ConvertKit, and Drip, that offer a range of features and integrations to help you automate your emails.

Segment your audience: Segment your audience based on their behavior, preferences, or other demographic information to ensure that each group of subscribers receives targeted, relevant messages.

Create your email templates: Write your automated email messages, keeping them short, sweet, and focused on your desired outcome.

Set up your triggers: Choose the specific actions or events that will trigger each automated email in your series, such as a subscriber joining your mailing list, or a customer purchasing a product.

Test your automation: Before launching your automated email campaign, test your emails to ensure that they are functioning correctly and that the content is appropriate for your audience.

Monitor your results: Regularly review the results of your automated email campaigns to measure their effectiveness and make any necessary adjustments.

By following these steps, you can automate your email campaigns and reach your target audience with consistent, personalized, and timely messages. With the right strategy, email automation can help you achieve your goals and grow your business.

CHAPTER 13 EMAIL MARKETING HACK #10: USE A DOUBLE OPT-IN

Explanation of double opt-in
Benefits of double opt-in
How to use double opt-in
Explanation of Double Opt-In

Double opt-in is a two-step process that helps to confirm that the recipient is genuinely interested in receiving emails from you. This process helps to reduce the number of people who mark your emails as spam and helps to maintain a clean email list of engaged subscribers.

The first step in the double opt-in process is to provide an email address and request to receive emails from you. The recipient provides their email address through a sign-up form on your website or through an opt-in button in one of your emails.

The second step is to confirm that the recipient wants to receive emails by clicking a confirmation link that is sent to the email address provided. The confirmation link takes the recipient to a page that confirms their subscription and allows them to start receiving your emails. This second step helps to ensure that the email address provided is accurate and that the recipient is genuinely interested in receiving your emails.

Double opt-in has several benefits for email marketers. By using double opt-in, you can maintain a clean email list of engaged subscribers. This helps to increase the effectiveness of your email marketing campaigns and ensures that your emails are delivered to people who are actually interested in receiving them. Additionally, using double opt-in can help to reduce the number of people who mark your emails as spam, which can help to improve your email deliverability and protect your sender reputation.

In conclusion, double opt-in is a useful tool for email marketers who want to maintain a clean email list of engaged subscribers and improve the effectiveness of their email marketing campaigns. By using double opt-in, you can ensure that your emails are delivered to people who are genuinely interested in receiving them, and you can reduce the number of people who mark your emails as spam.

Benefits of Double Opt-In

Additionally, using double opt-in can provide valuable data on the effectiveness of your email marketing campaigns. By tracking the number of people who opt-in and the number of people who confirm their email address, you can determine the overall interest in your content and make informed decisions about your email marketing strategy.

Finally, double opt-in helps to build trust with your audience. By demonstrating that you respect their privacy and are only sending emails to those who have explicitly requested them, you can establish a positive relationship with your subscribers and increase the chances of them becoming loyal customers.

In summary, double opt-in is an effective way to improve the quality of your email list, increase deliverability, reduce spam complaints, and improve engagement with your audience. By requiring confirmation of email addresses, you can ensure that your emails are being sent to people who are truly interested in your content, leading to more successful email marketing campaigns.

How to Use Double Opt-In

To use double opt-in for your email marketing campaigns, follow these steps:

Set up a sign-up form on your website or landing page where people can provide their email address and request to receive emails from you.

Use an email marketing service to send a confirmation email to the email address provided.

Include a confirmation link in the confirmation email that the recipient must click to confirm their email address.

Once the recipient has confirmed their email address, they will start receiving your emails.

By using double opt-in, you can ensure that your email marketing campaigns reach the right people and that they are interested in receiving your content. This will help to improve your email deliverability and engagement, leading to better results for your email marketing efforts.

CHAPTER 14 EMAIL MARKETING HACK #11: KEEP YOUR EMAIL LIST CLEAN

Explanation of clean email list
Benefits of clean email list
How to keep your email list clean

Email marketing is one of the most effective ways to reach and engage with your target audience. But, to achieve the best results, it's essential to maintain a clean and accurate email list. A clean email list is free from inactive or invalid email addresses and helps to ensure that your emails are delivered to the right people and that they are interested in your content.

In this chapter, we will explore the importance of keeping your email list clean and the benefits it can bring to your email marketing campaigns. We'll also look at how to keep your email list clean, including tips for removing inactive email addresses and maintaining an accurate email list. By the end of this chapter, you'll understand the significance of a clean email list and how it can help to improve the success of your email marketing campaigns.

Explanation of clean email list

A clean email list refers to a database of email addresses that is free from invalid, outdated, or undeliverable emails. A clean email list is important for email marketers as it helps to ensure that their emails are delivered to the right people and that they are not wasting time and resources sending emails to people who will never see them.

To maintain a clean email list, email marketers need to regularly check their database for invalid, outdated, or undeliverable email addresses. This can be done by using email verification software or by sending a test email to each address on the list. If an email is returned as undeliverable or if the recipient does not open the email, it is likely that the email address is no longer in use and should be removed from the list.

A clean email list not only improves the delivery rate of your emails, but it also helps to improve the overall quality of your email list and the success of your email marketing campaigns.

Benefits of clean email list

Having a clean email list is crucial for the success of your email marketing campaigns. A clean email list refers to an email list that is free from outdated or inaccurate information, and is composed of active, engaged subscribers. There are several benefits to keeping your email list clean, including:

Improved Deliverability: A clean email list means that your emails are more likely to reach the inbox of your subscribers, leading to higher open and click-through rates.

Reduced Spam Complaints: By sending emails only to active subscribers, you reduce the likelihood that your emails will be marked as spam, which can harm your sender reputation and reduce the deliverability of your future emails.

Increased Engagement: A clean email list ensures that you are communicating with people who are genuinely interested in your content, leading to improved engagement and better results from your email marketing campaigns.

Increased ROI: A clean email list leads to better email performance, which translates to higher return on investment for your email marketing efforts. By keeping your email list clean, you can maximize the value of your email marketing campaigns and achieve your desired results.

How to keep your email list clean

Keeping your email list clean is essential for the success of your email marketing campaigns. A clean email list is free from outdated, invalid, or inaccurate email addresses that could negatively impact your deliverability and reputation as a sender. By maintaining a clean email list, you can improve the effectiveness of your email marketing efforts, increase your open and click-through rates, and build stronger relationships with your subscribers.

To keep your email list clean, follow these steps:

Remove inactive subscribers: Regularly remove subscribers who have not engaged with your emails in a specified period of time. This helps to keep your email list updated and relevant.

Validate email addresses: Verify email addresses when they are collected and remove any invalid or inaccurate addresses. This helps to reduce the number of bounced emails and improve the deliverability of your campaigns.

Monitor bounce rates: Regularly monitor your bounce rates and remove any email addresses that are bouncing back. This helps to improve the deliverability of your campaigns and protect your sender reputation.

Remove duplicate email addresses: Remove any duplicate email addresses that may have been added to your list multiple times.

Regularly update your email list: Encourage your subscribers to update their email addresses if they change, and regularly clean up your list to ensure that it is up-to-date.

By following these steps, you can keep your email list clean and improve the effectiveness of your email marketing campaigns.

CHAPTER 15 EMAIL MARKETING HACK #12: USE A TRIGGERED WELCOME EMAIL

Explanation of triggered welcome email
Benefits of triggered welcome email
How to use triggered welcome email

Welcome to Chapter 15 of our email marketing guide, where we delve into the world of triggered welcome emails. Triggered welcome emails are an automated response sent to new subscribers as soon as they sign up for your email list. These emails serve as an introduction to your brand and set the tone for future communications.

In this chapter, we'll provide an in-depth explanation of triggered welcome emails, the benefits they offer, and tips on how to use them effectively. Whether you're just starting out with email marketing or looking to improve your existing strategy, this chapter is an essential read. So let's dive in and explore the power of triggered welcome emails!

Explanation of triggered welcome email

A triggered welcome email is an automated email that is sent to new subscribers as soon as they sign up to your email list. The main purpose of a triggered welcome email is to welcome the new subscriber, introduce your brand, and set the tone for future communications. This type of email can be highly effective in building a relationship with your new subscribers and increasing their engagement with your brand.

Triggered welcome emails are typically sent within the first few minutes or hours of a new subscriber signing up for your email list. They are highly personalized and often include a personalized greeting, information about your brand, and a call-to-action encouraging the subscriber to take further action, such as making a purchase or reading a blog post.

Triggered welcome emails can be customized to suit the needs of your business and target audience, and they can be designed to be simple and straightforward or more complex and interactive. Regardless of the design, the main goal of a triggered welcome email is to make a strong first impression with your new subscribers and build a relationship with them that will last.

Benefits of triggered welcome email

Welcome emails are the first touchpoint between a business and a new subscriber, making them a critical component of any email marketing strategy. Triggered welcome emails are a type of welcome email that are automatically sent to new subscribers as soon as they sign up for your email list. These emails are highly effective in building engagement, establishing a connection with your audience, and setting expectations for future communications.

There are several key benefits to using triggered welcome emails in your email marketing strategy, including:

Increased Open Rates: Welcome emails have a higher open rate compared to other types of emails. Triggered welcome emails capitalize on the initial excitement of a new subscriber and the timing is right, resulting in a higher open rate.

Improved Engagement: Triggered welcome emails help to establish a connection with your new subscribers, encouraging them to engage with your brand and content. This early engagement can lay the foundation for a long-term relationship.

Increased Brand Awareness: Welcome emails provide an opportunity to introduce your brand to new subscribers, reinforcing your messaging and showcasing your values and offerings.

Improved Deliverability: Triggered welcome emails help to establish your brand as a trusted sender in the eyes of email providers, reducing the likelihood that future emails will be marked as spam.

Increased Conversion Rates: Welcome emails can provide an immediate call-to-action, encouraging new subscribers to take their first step with your brand. This can result in increased conversion rates, driving sales and building your customer base.

Overall, triggered welcome emails are a simple and effective way to build engagement and establish a connection with your new subscribers. By capitalizing on the initial excitement of a new subscriber, you can create a strong foundation for a successful email marketing strategy.

Example of Using Triggered Welcome Email:

Subject Line: Welcome to [Brand Name]!

Dear [Name],

We're thrilled to have you on board as a new subscriber to [Brand Name]. Thank you for taking the time to sign up and join our community.

At [Brand Name], our goal is to provide you with valuable information and resources that can help you [insert goal/objective]. And as a welcome gift, we'd like to offer you a [insert incentive, such as a discount or free resource].

To claim your welcome gift, simply [insert instructions for claiming the offer].

Again, thank you for joining us, and we look forward to providing you with the best content and resources we have to offer.

Warm Regards,

[Your Name]

Example of Not Using Triggered Welcome Email:

Subject Line: [Brand Name] Newsletter

Dear [Name],

We're reaching out to share the latest news and updates from [Brand Name]. In this newsletter, you'll find [insert brief overview of content].

We hope you enjoy this edition of our newsletter, and as always, if you have any questions or feedback, please don't hesitate to reach out.

Best regards,

[Your Name]

As you can see, the first example includes a personalized greeting, thanks the subscriber for signing up, and offers a special welcome gift. The second example, on the other hand, is a generic newsletter without any personalization or welcome offer. By using a triggered welcome email, you can create a more personalized and engaging experience for new subscribers, helping to build a strong relationship with them from the start.

How to use triggered welcome email

Triggered welcome emails are automated messages that are sent to new subscribers as soon as they sign up for your email list. These emails are a great way to make a positive first impression on your new subscribers and start building a relationship with them. In this chapter, we will explore the steps you can take to set up and use triggered welcome emails effectively.

Step 1: Create a Welcome Email Campaign

The first step in using triggered welcome emails is to create an email campaign that will be sent to new subscribers. This email should be welcoming, informative, and set the tone for future emails. It should also include a clear call to action, such as asking subscribers to follow you on social media or visit your website.

Step 2: Choose an Email Service Provider

To send triggered welcome emails, you will need to use an email service provider. Some popular options include Mailchimp, Constant Contact, and Aweber. Choose the one that best fits your needs and budget, and sign up for an account.

Step 3: Set Up an Automated Workflow

Once you have chosen your email service provider, you can set up an automated workflow that will send your welcome email to new subscribers. To do this, you will need to create a new automation rule, set the trigger to be a new subscriber, and then select the welcome email campaign you created in step 1 as the email to be sent.

Step 4: Test Your Triggered Welcome Email

Before you start sending your triggered welcome email, be sure to test it thoroughly. Send a test email to yourself and check that the email looks and functions as you intended. You may also want to consider having someone else test it to make sure it is working properly.

Step 5: Monitor and Refine Your Triggered Welcome Email

Once your triggered welcome email is live, monitor its performance and refine it as needed. Look at metrics such as open rates, click-through rates, and conversion rates, and make changes to your email if you notice any areas for improvement.

In conclusion, using a triggered welcome email is a great way to make a positive first impression on your new subscribers and start building a relationship with them. By following the steps outlined in this chapter, you can set up and use triggered welcome emails effectively, and start seeing the benefits for yourself.

CHAPTER 16 EMAIL MARKETING HACK #13: USE A/B TESTING

Explanation of A/B testing
Benefits of A/B testing
How to use A/B testing

A/B testing is an essential tool for any successful email marketing campaign. It's a simple yet effective way to compare two versions of an email to determine which one performs better. This technique allows you to make data-driven decisions about your email content and design, improving the overall performance of your campaigns and helping you achieve your goals.

In this chapter, we will delve into the explanation of A/B testing, the benefits it provides, and how to use it effectively. Whether you're a seasoned email marketer or just starting out, A/B testing is a powerful tool that can help you optimize your campaigns and take your email marketing to the next level. So buckle up and get ready to learn how to harness the power of A/B testing in your email marketing campaigns.

Explanation of A/B testing

A/B testing is a popular method for improving the performance of email marketing campaigns. It is a method of comparing two variations of an email to determine which one performs better. The goal of A/B testing is to find the optimal design, subject line, or message that resonates best with your target audience, leading to better engagement and conversion rates.

A/B testing is a controlled experiment in which two or more variations of an email are sent to a sample of your email list. The variations can include different subject lines, calls-to-action, or layouts, among others. The email that performs the best is then sent to the rest of the list.

A/B testing helps to identify what works and what doesn't in your email marketing campaigns, allowing you to make informed decisions and improve your results over time. It is an ongoing process, as you continually test and refine your emails to optimize their performance.

It is important to note that A/B testing should not be limited to just the subject line or the call-to-action. The content of the email and the design elements should also be tested to determine their impact on the overall performance of your emails. By continuously testing and refining your emails, you can ensure that you are getting the most out of your email marketing efforts.

Benefits of A/B testing

A/B testing is a powerful tool in the arsenal of any email marketer. It allows you to test different aspects of your emails and determine what works best with your audience. The benefits of A/B testing are numerous and can help you to optimize your email campaigns for maximum results.

Improved Open and Click-Through Rates: By testing different subject lines, email designs, and content, you can identify the elements that resonate best with your audience and improve your open and click-through rates.

Increased Engagement: A/B testing can help you to determine what type of content your audience is most interested in and how to structure your emails for maximum engagement.

Better Deliverability: By testing different aspects of your emails, you can identify any factors that may be affecting your deliverability and make necessary changes to ensure that your emails reach your audience.

Increased Conversion Rates: A/B testing can help you to determine what elements of your emails are driving conversions and how you can optimize them for maximum results.

Data-Driven Decision Making: A/B testing provides you with hard data that can help you to make informed decisions about your email campaigns. This data can be used to guide your future email strategies and optimize your results.

In summary, the benefits of A/B testing are numerous and can help you to optimize your email campaigns for maximum results. By testing different aspects of your emails and using the data to guide your future strategies, you can achieve better engagement, higher conversion rates, and improved deliverability.

How to use A/B testing

A/B testing, also known as split testing, is a powerful tool for optimizing your email marketing campaigns. It involves creating two different versions of an email, with small variations, and then sending each version to a portion of your email list. By comparing the performance of the two versions, you can determine which version is more effective and then use that version for future email campaigns.

Here are the steps to use A/B testing for your email marketing campaigns:

Choose the Variable to Test: Choose the element of your email that you want to test. It could be the subject line, the call-to-action, the email design, or any other element that you think could impact the performance of your email.

Create Two Versions of Your Email: Once you have selected the variable to test, create two versions of your email, with the only difference being the variable you selected.

Determine the Sample Size: Decide how many people you want to send each version of your email to. A general rule of thumb is to have at least 100-200 people in each group.

Send the Emails: Send both versions of the email to the respective groups of people. It's important to send the emails at the same time to ensure that the results are accurate.

Analyze the Results: After the emails have been sent, analyze the results to determine which version performed better. You can use metrics such as open rates, click-through rates, and conversion rates to determine the success of each version.

Implement the Winning Version: Once you have determined which version performed better, use that version for future email campaigns. You can also use the insights from your A/B testing to make further improvements to your emails.

By using A/B testing, you can optimize your email marketing campaigns and ensure that your emails are as effective as possible. Whether you are a seasoned marketer or just starting out, A/B testing is a valuable tool that can help you improve your results and reach your email marketing goals.

Example of Using A/B Testing:

Suppose you are an e-commerce store that wants to increase sales through email marketing. You have been sending out emails to your subscribers, but you're not quite sure what type of content or subject line will lead to the highest open and click-through rates. To determine the most effective approach, you can use A/B testing.

You start by dividing your email list into two groups, with each group receiving a slightly different email. For example, you might send one email with a subject line that says "New arrivals: Check out our latest products!" to Group A and another email with a subject line that says "Exclusive offer: Get 20% off your first purchase!" to Group B.

After a few days, you compare the open and click-through rates for both emails. If you find that Group B has higher open and click-through rates, you can conclude that the subject line "Exclusive offer: Get 20% off your first purchase!" is more effective. In the future, you can use this information to create similar subject lines for your emails.

Example of Not Using A/B Testing:

Suppose you are a business that wants to improve your email marketing campaigns. However, you are not using A/B testing and are instead sending the same email to your entire email list without any modifications.

After a few weeks, you notice that your open and click-through rates are not as high as you had hoped. You are not sure what's causing this, so you continue to send the same email without making any changes.

Without A/B testing, you are not able to determine what elements of your email are not resonating with your subscribers. You could be missing out on potential opportunities to improve your open and click-through rates, leading to lower sales and revenue.

CHAPTER 17 EMAIL MARKETING HACK #14: SEND EMAILS AT THE RIGHT TIME

Explanation of sending emails at the right time
Benefits of sending emails at the right time
How to send emails at the right time

Email marketing is an effective way to reach your target audience and drive engagement. However, for your email campaigns to be successful, it's important to send your emails at the right time. Timing can play a critical role in the success of your email marketing campaigns. If you send your emails at the wrong time, they may go unnoticed or be marked as spam. In this chapter, we will explore the explanation of sending emails at the right time, the benefits of doing so, and how to ensure you are sending your emails at the right time.

Explanation of sending emails at the right time

Sending emails at the right time is a crucial aspect of email marketing that can have a significant impact on the success of your campaigns. It's about understanding the behavior and preferences of your audience and timing your emails accordingly.

The right time to send emails will vary based on a number of factors, including the type of business you run, the type of audience you are targeting, and the goals of your email campaign. For example, if you run a B2B company, you may want to send emails during the workweek when your audience is most likely to be checking their email. On the other hand, if you run a B2C company, you may want to send emails on weekends when people have more free time.

It's important to note that there is no one-size-fits-all answer to when the right time to send emails is. It's about testing and finding the best time for your specific audience. The best way to determine the right time to send emails is by testing and analyzing the open rates and engagement of your campaigns at different times. This will help you to identify the most effective time to send emails and optimize your email marketing strategy accordingly.

Benefits of sending emails at the right time

Sending emails at the right time can greatly impact the success of your email marketing campaigns. Timing can be the difference between a recipient ignoring your email or taking action and engaging with your brand. Here are some of the key benefits of sending emails at the right time:

Increased Open Rates: Sending emails at the right time can increase the likelihood that your recipients will open and engage with your email. This can lead to higher click-through rates and conversions.

Better Engagement: By sending emails when your recipients are most likely to be available and attentive, you can improve the quality of engagement with your brand. This can lead to higher open and click-through rates, as well as more conversions.

More Effective Targeting: Timing is an important factor when targeting specific audiences. By sending emails at the right time for your target audience, you can improve the chances of your email being seen and engaged with.

Improved Customer Relationships: Sending emails at the right time can help to build and maintain strong relationships with your customers. By demonstrating that you understand their preferences and are considerate of their time, you can improve customer loyalty and trust.

In summary, sending emails at the right time can greatly impact the success of your email marketing campaigns. It can increase open and engagement rates, improve targeting, and build stronger relationships with your customers.

How to send emails at the right time

The right time to send an email can vary depending on a number of factors, such as the recipient's location, their preferred communication style, and their schedule. However, here are some general tips for determining the right time to send an email:

Consider the recipient's time zone: If your email recipients are located in different time zones, consider the best time to reach them based on their location.

Test sending at different times: Try sending emails at different times of the day and track open rates to determine the best time to send.

Take into account work schedules: Weekdays during normal business hours are often the best times to send emails, as people are more likely to be checking their inboxes.

Consider the content of the email: If the email is time-sensitive, such as a sale or event, it's best to send it during business hours when the recipient is more likely to be available.

Personalize the send time: Some email marketing platforms allow you to personalize the send time for each recipient based on their individual behavior and preferences.

Ultimately, the right time to send an email will depend on your specific audience and goals, so it's important to test and continuously evaluate the results to determine the best approach for your campaigns.

CHAPTER 18 USE SEGMENTATION FOR BETTER TARGETING

Segment your email list based on subscriber preferences and behaviors

Target your audience with more personalized and relevant emails

Improve open rates, click-through rates, and overall engagement

Email marketing can be a highly effective way to reach your audience and promote your products or services, but to get the best results, you need to target your emails to the right people. That's where email segmentation comes in. Segmentation is the process of dividing your email list into smaller groups based on common characteristics, such as subscriber preferences or behaviors. By segmenting your email list, you can send more personalized and relevant emails that are tailored to the specific needs and interests of each group, resulting in improved open rates, click-through rates, and overall engagement. In this chapter, we'll explore the benefits of email segmentation and how to use it to reach your target audience with the right message, at the right time.

Segment your email list based on subscriber preferences and behaviors

Email segmentation is the process of dividing your email list into smaller groups based on specific criteria, such as subscriber preferences and behaviors. By doing this, you can send targeted and personalized emails to each segment, rather than sending a generic email to your entire email list. This leads to a better overall email experience for your subscribers and can result in improved engagement with your emails.

There are many different ways to segment your email list, but some of the most common include:

Demographic segmentation: Segmenting your email list based on demographic information, such as age, gender, location, and income.

Behavioral segmentation: Segmenting your email list based on subscriber behavior, such as their engagement with your emails, website, and social media.

Interest segmentation: Segmenting your email list based on subscriber interests, such as topics they are interested in, products they have purchased, and events they have attended.

Subscriber lifecycle segmentation: Segmenting your email list based on the stage of the subscriber lifecycle, such as new subscribers, inactive subscribers, and loyal subscribers.

By segmenting your email list, you can send targeted and relevant emails to each segment, which can lead to higher open rates, click-through rates, and overall engagement. Additionally, by tailoring your emails to the specific needs and interests of each segment, you can build stronger relationships with your subscribers and foster loyalty.

Target your audience with more personalized and relevant emails

Email segmentation is a powerful tool for making your email marketing campaigns more targeted and effective. By dividing your email list into smaller, more specific groups, you can send emails that are better tailored to the individual preferences and behaviors of each group. This, in turn, leads to higher open rates, click-through rates, and overall engagement.

Personalization is key when it comes to email marketing. By sending emails that are relevant and tailored to the recipient's interests, you are more likely to capture their attention and engage them. There are several ways you can segment your email list based on subscriber preferences and behaviors, including:

Demographic information: This includes data such as age, gender, location, and job title.

Purchase history: This can include data on the products or services that a subscriber has purchased in the past, as well as the frequency and amount of their purchases.

Behavioral data: This can include data on how subscribers interact with your emails, such as open and click-through rates, as well as the pages they visit on your website.

By using this data to create targeted email segments, you can send emails that are more relevant and personalized to each group. For example, if you have a group of subscribers who have purchased a particular product in the past, you can send them emails that promote related products or services. Alternatively, if you have a group of subscribers who frequently engage with your emails, you can send them special promotions or exclusive content to keep them interested.

In conclusion, targeting your audience with more personalized and relevant emails is a key strategy for improving the effectiveness of your email marketing campaigns. By segmenting your email list based on subscriber preferences and behaviors, you can create emails that are tailored to the individual needs and interests of each group, leading to higher open rates, click-through rates, and overall engagement.

CHAPTER 19 INCLUDE A STRONG CALL-TO-ACTION

Clearly state the desired action for the subscriber
Make it easy for the subscriber to take action
Use action-oriented language and attention-grabbing visuals

In the world of email marketing, a strong call-to-action (CTA) can make all the difference. A well-crafted CTA can not only increase engagement but also drive conversions and boost sales. Whether you want subscribers to make a purchase, sign up for a newsletter, or simply read your latest blog post, a clear and compelling CTA is an essential element of any effective email campaign.

In this chapter, we'll delve into the best practices for crafting strong CTAs, including how to clearly state the desired action, make it easy for subscribers to take that action, and use action-oriented language and attention-grabbing visuals to grab the recipient's attention. With the right approach and attention to detail, you can create CTAs that help you achieve your email marketing goals and drive success for your business.

Clearly state the desired action for the subscriber

One of the most important elements of a successful email marketing campaign is a strong call-to-action (CTA). A CTA is a statement or button that prompts the recipient to take a specific action, such as making a purchase, signing up for a newsletter, or downloading a resource. To ensure that your CTA is effective, it's important to clearly state the desired action.

When crafting your CTA, be clear and concise about what you want the subscriber to do. Don't use vague or ambiguous language, as this can confuse the reader and cause them to ignore your CTA altogether. Instead, use action-oriented language that clearly communicates the desired outcome. For example, instead of saying "Learn More," say "Download Our Ebook."

It's also important to make sure that your CTA is prominent and easy to find within the body of your email. Place it in a location where it can be easily seen and clicked, such as above the fold or near the end of the email. Use attention-grabbing visuals, such as bold text, bright colors, and eye-catching graphics, to make your CTA stand out and draw the reader's eye.

In conclusion, by clearly stating the desired action and making it easy to find and click, you can increase the effectiveness of your CTA and drive more conversions.

Make it easy for the subscriber to take action

A strong call-to-action is essential to the success of your email marketing campaigns. However, the strength of the call-to-action depends on how easy it is for the subscriber to take action. When designing your call-to-action, it is important to make the desired action simple and straightforward for the subscriber. This will encourage them to take the next step and engage with your brand.

There are several ways to make it easy for the subscriber to take action:

Keep the call-to-action button prominent: The call-to-action button should be visually prominent, standing out from the rest of the email content. It should also be placed in a location where the subscriber can easily find it, such as at the top or bottom of the email.

Use action-oriented language: The language used in the call-to-action should be action-oriented and clear, encouraging the subscriber to take the desired action. For example, instead of using the words "click here", use "Sign up now" or "Get started today".

Make the desired action easy to complete: The desired action should be easy to complete, taking no more than a few clicks. The process should be streamlined and straightforward, so the subscriber can take the desired action without feeling frustrated or overwhelmed.

Test and optimize: Regularly test different aspects of the call-to-action, such as the language, button placement, and desired action, to determine what works best for your audience. Use the data collected from these tests to optimize future campaigns and make it even easier for the subscriber to take action.

By making it easy for the subscriber to take action, you can increase the effectiveness of your email marketing campaigns and drive better engagement with your brand.

Use action-oriented language and attention-grabbing visuals

One of the most important aspects of a successful email marketing campaign is having a strong call-to-action (CTA). A CTA is the instruction or prompt that you give to your subscribers to take a specific action, such as making a purchase, filling out a form, or visiting a website. To be effective, your CTA needs to be clear, easy to follow, and visually appealing.

Action-oriented language and attention-grabbing visuals are two key elements of a strong CTA. The language you use should be direct and tell the subscriber exactly what you want them to do, using action verbs like "click," "download," or "register." Avoid vague language and keep your CTA simple and to the point.

In addition to using action-oriented language, your CTA should also be visually appealing and stand out from the rest of your email content. Use contrasting colors, bold fonts, or an attention-grabbing image to draw the subscriber's eye to your CTA. Make sure that your CTA is easy to find and that it is placed in a prominent location, such as above the fold or at the end of your email.

By incorporating action-oriented language and attention-grabbing visuals into your email campaigns, you can increase the effectiveness of your CTAs and drive more conversions. Always test and optimize your CTAs to see what works best for your audience and make changes accordingly. Remember, a strong CTA is an essential component of a successful email marketing campaign, so make sure to give it the attention it deserves.

Example email using the information from this chapter:

Subject: Don't Miss Out on 20% off Your Next Purchase!

Dear [Name],

We're thrilled to offer you a special discount on your next purchase! For a limited time, use the code 20OFF at checkout and get 20% off your order.

But hurry, this offer expires in just 48 hours. So, what are you waiting for? Treat yourself to something new today!

[CTA Button] Shop Now

Thank you for being a valued customer. We appreciate your business and look forward to serving you again soon.

Best regards,

[Your Name]

Example email not using the information from this chapter:

Subject: Latest Updates

Hi [Name],

Just wanted to let you know about our latest updates. We have a lot of new arrivals and promotions. Check them out if you get a chance.

Thanks,

[Your Name]

As you can see, the second example lacks a clear call-to-action and doesn't use action-oriented language or attention-grabbing visuals. The first email, on the other hand, clearly states the desired action (to use the code and get 20% off), makes it easy for the subscriber to take action (with the CTA button), and uses attention-grabbing language (limited time offer).

CHAPTER 20 TRACK AND ANALYZE YOUR RESULTS

Use email marketing analytics to track the performance of your campaigns

Measure open rates, click-through rates, conversions, and other important metrics

Use this data to continuously improve your email marketing strategy

Email marketing can be an effective tool for reaching and engaging with your target audience, but it's important to know how well your campaigns are performing. That's where tracking and analyzing your results comes in. By keeping an eye on key metrics, you can see what's working, what's not, and make data-driven decisions to optimize your strategy and improve your results. In this chapter, we'll discuss the importance of using email marketing analytics, the metrics to track, and how to use the data to continually improve your email marketing efforts.

Use email marketing analytics to track the performance of your campaigns

Measure open rates, click-through rates, conversions, and other important metrics

Use this data to continuously improve your email marketing strategy

Use email marketing analytics to track the performance of your campaigns

One of the most important aspects of successful email marketing is tracking and analyzing the results of your campaigns. By using email marketing analytics, you can measure key metrics such as open rates, click-through rates, conversions, and more. This data provides valuable insights into the performance of your campaigns and allows you to make informed decisions about how to improve your email marketing strategy.

Email marketing analytics tools allow you to track important metrics such as:

Open rates: This metric measures the percentage of people who opened your email. It gives you an idea of how many people are interested in your content and whether or not they are engaged with your brand.
Click-through rates: This metric measures the percentage of people who clicked on a link in your email. It helps you understand how well your email content resonates with your audience and whether or not it is effectively driving them to take action.
Conversions: This metric measures the number of people who completed a desired action, such as making a purchase or filling out a form. It helps you understand how well your email campaigns are driving sales and leads.
By using email marketing analytics, you can gain valuable insights into the performance of your campaigns and make informed decisions about how to improve your email marketing strategy. Whether you are looking to increase open rates, drive more sales, or build better relationships with your subscribers, email marketing analytics is a critical tool for success.

Measure open rates, click-through rates, conversions, and other important metrics

When it comes to analyzing the success of your email marketing campaigns, there are a number of metrics that you need to be aware of. Open rates, click-through rates, and conversions are among the most important metrics to track.

Open rates give you an idea of how many people are actually opening your emails. This metric can help you understand if your subject lines are effectively grabbing people's attention, or if your subscribers are losing interest in your emails. To calculate your open rate, simply divide the number of people who opened your email by the number of people who received it.

Click-through rates, on the other hand, measure the number of people who clicked on links within your email. This metric is an indicator of how engaging your content is and how effectively you are guiding people to take action. To calculate your click-through rate, divide the number of clicks by the number of opens.

Conversions are the ultimate goal of any marketing campaign, and email marketing is no exception. A conversion is defined as a desired action taken by the subscriber, such as making a purchase or filling out a form. Tracking conversions will give you an idea of how effective your emails are in actually driving results.

Other important metrics to track include bounce rate, unsubscribe rate, and complaint rate. Bounce rate measures the number of emails that couldn't be delivered to subscribers, while unsubscribe rate measures the number of people who opt-out of receiving future emails from you. Complaint rate measures the number of emails marked as spam by subscribers.

By regularly tracking and analyzing these metrics, you can make data-driven decisions to continuously improve your email marketing strategy.

CHAPTER 23 CONCLUSION:

Email marketing is a crucial component of modern digital marketing strategies. Throughout this book, we have explored various email marketing hacks that businesses can use to improve their email campaigns and achieve better results. In this concluding chapter, we will summarize the key points covered in the previous chapters, emphasize the importance of email marketing, and encourage the reader to implement the hacks discussed to achieve success with their email marketing efforts. By following the strategies outlined in this book, businesses can leverage the power of email to connect with their audience, build brand awareness, drive engagement and sales, and achieve long-term success.

In this chapter, we will summarize the main points covered in the previous chapters of the book. Email marketing is an important aspect of a successful business strategy and can have a significant impact on a company's bottom line. Throughout this book, we have discussed various email marketing hacks that can help businesses improve the effectiveness of their email campaigns and achieve success.

We started by discussing the importance of building a clean email list and the benefits of keeping the list up-to-date and accurate. We then covered the benefits of using a triggered welcome email and how to effectively implement this hack.

We also discussed the importance of A/B testing, and the benefits it can bring to your email marketing efforts. We covered how to use A/B testing to optimize your email campaigns and improve their effectiveness.

We also looked at the benefits of sending emails at the right time and provided some tips on how to determine the best times to send your emails.

We talked about the importance of segmenting your email list and how it can help you target your audience more effectively with more personalized and relevant emails. We also covered the importance of testing and optimizing your email campaigns and how to use the data collected to refine your email marketing strategy.

Finally, we discussed the importance of tracking and analyzing the results of your email campaigns, including open rates, click-through rates, conversions, and other important metrics.

In conclusion, email marketing can have a huge impact on a business's success, and by following the hacks outlined in this book, you can improve the effectiveness of your email campaigns and achieve the results you desire. So take the time to implement these hacks and see what a difference they can make for your business.

PART 3 GAME CHANGER SALES SOLUTION

CHAPTER 24 GAME CHANGER SALES SOLUTION

In the ever-evolving digital landscape, it's important for businesses to stay ahead of the curve and make the most of the latest marketing strategies and technologies. In this chapter, we'll explore a range of game-changing sales solutions that can help businesses reach new audiences, drive growth, and increase sales. From social media marketing to video marketing, we'll discuss the different platforms and techniques available, as well as the benefits and potential impact each can have on a business. Whether you're new to digital marketing or looking to optimize your existing efforts, this chapter will provide you with a comprehensive overview of the key strategies and tools available to take your business to the next level.

Social Media Marketing - Discuss the various platforms (e.g. Facebook, Instagram, Twitter) and how to use them effectively to reach your target audience.

Social media marketing has become an essential component of any comprehensive marketing strategy. With over 3.8 billion people worldwide using social media platforms, the potential reach for businesses is enormous. Some of the most popular social media platforms include Facebook, Instagram, and Twitter. These platforms can be used effectively to reach your target audience, engage with them, and drive conversions.

Facebook has over 2.8 billion monthly active users, making it the largest social media platform in the world. Facebook allows businesses to create pages, run ads, and interact with customers through posts and comments. Instagram is a photo and video sharing platform with over 1 billion monthly active users. Instagram allows businesses to share visually appealing content and reach new audiences through hashtags and influencer marketing. Twitter is a micro-blogging platform with over 330 million monthly active users. Twitter allows businesses to reach their target audience through tweets and engage with them in real-time through direct messaging and retweets.

To effectively use social media platforms to reach your target audience, it's important to understand the audience and their behavior on each platform. This includes understanding what type of content resonates with them, what type of messaging they respond to, and what time of day they are most active. By leveraging this information, businesses can create and share content that resonates with their target audience and drive engagement.

It's also important to utilize tools and technologies to effectively manage your social media presence. This includes scheduling tools to automate the publishing of content, analytics tools to track the performance of your posts, and monitoring tools to track and respond to customer comments and feedback.

In conclusion, social media marketing is a powerful tool for businesses to reach their target audience, engage with them, and drive conversions. By understanding the audience and their behavior on each platform and utilizing the right tools and technologies, businesses can maximize their results and achieve success with their social media marketing efforts.

Content Marketing - Discuss the importance of creating valuable, relevant and engaging content to attract and retain customers.

Content marketing is a strategy that focuses on creating and sharing valuable, relevant, and engaging content with the goal of attracting and retaining a clearly defined target audience. By providing useful information, solving problems, and addressing the needs of your audience, content marketing can help you establish your business as a trusted and authoritative source. In turn, this can lead to increased customer loyalty, brand awareness, and ultimately, sales.

There are many different types of content you can create as part of your content marketing strategy, including blog posts, videos, infographics, case studies, whitepapers, and more. The key is to choose formats that align with your target audience's preferences and needs, and to ensure that your content is high-quality and provides value to the reader.

In addition to creating great content, it's also important to promote it effectively. This may involve leveraging social media, email marketing, search engine optimization (SEO), and other channels to reach your target audience.

To be successful with content marketing, it's crucial to have a clear understanding of your target audience, their needs, and the types of content they are looking for. By delivering valuable and relevant content that resonates with your audience, you can build a loyal following, increase brand awareness, and drive real business results.

Influencer Marketing - Discuss how to identify and collaborate with influencers to reach new audiences and grow your business.

Influencer marketing is a popular and effective marketing strategy that involves partnering with individuals who have a significant following on social media to promote a product, service, or brand. Influencer marketing has become increasingly popular in recent years, as businesses look for new and innovative ways to reach their target audience and stand out from the competition. In this chapter, we'll discuss how to identify and collaborate with influencers to reach new audiences and grow your business.

Finding Influencers

The first step in influencer marketing is finding the right influencer to partner with. This can be done by looking at their social media profiles and assessing their followers, engagement rate, and overall fit with your brand. When choosing an influencer, it's important to consider their niche, the type of content they create, and their values and beliefs. It's also a good idea to work with influencers who have a similar target audience to your own, as this will help ensure that their followers are more likely to be interested in your product or service.

Working with Influencers

Once you've found the right influencer, it's time to start collaborating. This can involve working with them to create sponsored content, offering them a discount on your product or service, or giving them early access to new products or features. When working with influencers, it's important to be clear about your expectations and to set clear goals for the partnership. It's also important to be transparent about your compensation and to ensure that the influencer fully understands the terms of the agreement.

Measuring Success

Finally, it's important to measure the success of your influencer marketing efforts. This can be done by tracking metrics such as reach, engagement, and conversions. By monitoring these metrics, you'll be able to see what's working and what's not, and you can use this information to make informed decisions about your future influencer marketing campaigns.

In conclusion, influencer marketing is a powerful marketing tool that can help you reach new audiences and grow your business. By partnering with the right influencer and using clear, transparent communication, you can create successful campaigns that drive results and help you stand out from the competition.

Search Engine Optimization (SEO) - Discuss the strategies and techniques for improving your website's ranking in search engines.

Search Engine Optimization (SEO) is a crucial aspect of digital marketing, as it helps businesses improve their website's visibility and ranking in search engine results pages (SERPs). SEO helps to attract organic traffic to your website, which can lead to increased leads, sales, and brand recognition.

There are several strategies and techniques that businesses can use to improve their SEO. Some of the most important ones include:

Keyword research: This involves identifying the keywords and phrases that potential customers are searching for and optimizing your website content to target those keywords.

On-page optimization: This involves optimizing the content and structure of your website to improve its relevance and authority for target keywords. This includes optimizing your website's title tags, meta descriptions, headings, and images.

Technical SEO: This involves optimizing the technical elements of your website, such as its URL structure, website speed, and mobile responsiveness, to ensure that search engines can easily crawl and index your content.

Link building: This involves acquiring high-quality backlinks from other websites to your website. Backlinks act as a vote of confidence in your website, helping to improve its authority and ranking in search engine results pages.

Content creation: This involves creating high-quality, relevant, and engaging content that provides value to your target audience. This can include blog posts, infographics, videos, and other types of content that are optimized for target keywords.

By implementing these strategies and techniques, businesses can improve their SEO and achieve higher visibility and ranking in search engine results pages. This can lead to increased organic traffic, leads, and sales, and help to establish your business as an authority in your industry.

Pay-per-click (PPC) advertising - Discuss how to use paid advertising to drive traffic to your website and increase conversions.

Pay-per-click (PPC) advertising is a powerful marketing strategy that allows businesses to reach their target audience through paid online advertising. The main goal of PPC advertising is to drive traffic to a website and increase conversions, such as sales or leads.

One of the biggest benefits of PPC advertising is its flexibility and scalability. PPC campaigns can be easily adjusted based on the results, so businesses can quickly change their approach if the results are not meeting their expectations. Additionally, PPC advertising can be scaled up or down depending on the budget, making it a cost-effective option for businesses of all sizes.

To get started with PPC advertising, businesses need to first identify their target audience and determine the keywords that their target audience is searching for. Next, businesses should create compelling ads that accurately represent their products or services and that will catch the attention of their target audience.

One of the most popular platforms for PPC advertising is Google AdWords, which allows businesses to target their ads to specific audiences and geographic locations. Another popular platform is Facebook Ads, which allows businesses to target their ads based on specific interests, behaviors, and demographic information.

In order to ensure that their PPC advertising campaigns are effective, businesses should regularly monitor their performance and adjust their strategy as needed. This may involve tweaking their ads, changing their target audience, or adjusting their budget.

In conclusion, PPC advertising is a powerful marketing tool that can help businesses reach their target audience and increase conversions. By following a well-planned strategy and continuously monitoring and adjusting their campaigns, businesses can achieve success with their PPC advertising efforts.

Conversion Rate Optimization (CRO) - Discuss the techniques and tools used to increase the conversion rate of your website.

Conversion Rate Optimization (CRO) is a process that involves using data, testing, and customer insights to improve the performance of your website and increase the rate at which visitors convert into customers. The ultimate goal of CRO is to turn more visitors into customers by making the website experience as seamless, engaging, and relevant as possible.

One of the most important aspects of CRO is data analysis. By tracking and analyzing the behavior of your website visitors, you can gain insights into what is working well and what needs improvement. From this data, you can make informed decisions about which changes to make to your website to optimize the conversion rate.

Once you have analyzed the data, it's time to start testing. There are many different types of tests that you can run to improve the conversion rate of your website, including A/B testing, multivariate testing, and heat mapping. A/B testing involves testing two variations of a page to see which one performs better, while multivariate testing involves testing multiple variables at the same time. Heat mapping is a visual representation of where users are clicking on your website.

Another key aspect of CRO is improving the user experience. This can be achieved by making sure the website is easy to navigate, the content is engaging and relevant, and the overall design is visually appealing. Additionally, you can use tools like customer feedback forms and live chat to gather insights from your customers about what they like and dislike about your website.

Finally, it is important to continuously monitor and optimize your website. CRO is not a one-time process, but rather a continuous cycle of data analysis, testing, and optimization. By regularly monitoring your website's performance and making changes based on the data, you can continuously improve the conversion rate and drive more sales for your business.

In conclusion, Conversion Rate Optimization (CRO) is a crucial aspect of online marketing and can greatly impact the success of your business. By utilizing data analysis, testing, user experience optimization, and continuous monitoring, you can optimize your website for maximum conversions and achieve your business goals.

Mobile Marketing - Discuss the importance of mobile optimization and the various strategies for reaching customers on mobile devices.

Mobile devices are now an integral part of our daily lives, and it is essential for businesses to have a mobile-optimized presence. The majority of internet users access the web through their smartphones, and it has become critical for businesses to reach their target audience through these devices. In this chapter, we will discuss the importance of mobile optimization and the various strategies for reaching customers on mobile devices.

The Importance of Mobile Optimization

In today's world, people are constantly on the go and expect to have access to information and services through their mobile devices. A mobile-optimized website is essential for providing a seamless and user-friendly experience to your target audience. If your website is not optimized for mobile, visitors are likely to leave and seek out a competitor's website that provides a better experience. This can result in a loss of potential customers and revenue.

Moreover, search engines, such as Google, now prioritize mobile-optimized websites in their search results. This means that a mobile-optimized website is more likely to rank higher in search results, increasing its visibility and reach.

Strategies for Reaching Customers on Mobile Devices

Mobile-Optimized Website

A mobile-optimized website is a must for reaching customers on mobile devices. Your website should be designed to adjust its layout and content based on the size of the device it is being viewed on. This includes using a responsive design, large font sizes, and a simple, easy-to-use navigation system.

Mobile Apps

Mobile apps provide a more engaging and personalized experience for your customers. Apps can be used for a variety of purposes, such as e-commerce, booking appointments, and providing access to exclusive content. By offering a mobile app, businesses can reach their target audience where they spend the most time – on their mobile devices.

SMS Marketing

SMS marketing is a powerful tool for reaching customers on mobile devices. SMS messages have a high open rate, and customers are more likely to respond to a text message compared to an email. This makes SMS marketing a great way to send time-sensitive messages and promotions to your target audience.

Mobile Advertising

Mobile advertising is another effective way to reach customers on mobile devices. Platforms such as Facebook, Google, and Instagram offer a range of mobile advertising options, such as display ads, video ads, and sponsored content. By targeting your ads to the right audience and using engaging visuals, mobile advertising can drive traffic to your website and increase conversions.

In conclusion, mobile optimization and the various strategies for reaching customers on mobile devices are essential for businesses to reach their target audience and remain competitive in today's market. By implementing these strategies, businesses can improve their visibility, reach, and engagement with their target audience on mobile devices.

Video Marketing - Discuss the benefits of using video as a marketing tool and the various types of video content you can create.

Video marketing is an increasingly popular and effective way to reach and engage with your target audience. By using moving images, sound, and a creative storyline, you can create an experience that captures the viewer's attention and delivers a memorable message. With the rise of platforms such as YouTube, Vimeo, and TikTok, it has never been easier to share your videos with a wide audience.

The Benefits of Video Marketing

There are numerous benefits to incorporating video marketing into your overall marketing strategy. Firstly, video is a highly engaging form of content, with viewers often more likely to watch and retain the information presented in a video than they are to read a blog post or article. Secondly, video provides a flexible format that can be used in a variety of different ways, such as product demos, company culture videos, customer testimonials, and more.

In addition, video provides a unique opportunity to build a personal connection with your audience. By creating videos that showcase your brand's personality and values, you can build a strong relationship with your audience and create a sense of trust and loyalty. Furthermore, video provides a valuable opportunity to educate and inform your audience, delivering information in an entertaining and engaging way.

Types of Video Content

There are many different types of video content that you can create, each with their own specific benefits and purposes. Some of the most common types of video content include:

Product demos – Showcasing your products in action is a powerful way to demonstrate their value and build excitement among potential customers.

Company culture videos – Give your audience a behind-the-scenes look at your company and show off the values and personality of your brand.

Customer testimonials – Let your happy customers speak for you, sharing their experiences and why they choose your brand.

How-to videos – Teach your audience something new and demonstrate your expertise in a particular subject.

Animated explainer videos – Use animation to simplify complex concepts and make them easier for your audience to understand.

By creating a variety of different video content, you can reach your audience in new and exciting ways and keep them engaged with your brand.

Tips for Creating Effective Video Content

To create effective video content, it's important to keep the following tips in mind:

Know your audience – What type of content will they find most valuable and engaging?

Be clear and concise – Keep your videos short and focused, delivering one key message per video.

Use high-quality equipment – Invest in good lighting, sound, and camera equipment to create professional-looking videos.

Add subtitles – Subtitles help to make your videos more accessible and increase engagement.

Optimize for different platforms – Each video platform has its own specific requirements, so be sure to optimize your videos for each platform you use.

By using video marketing, you can reach and engage with your audience in new and exciting ways, building stronger relationships and driving more sales.

Affiliate Marketing - Discuss how to leverage the power of affiliates to promote your products or services and increase sales.

Affiliate marketing is a cost-effective and results-driven marketing strategy that involves partnering with other businesses to promote your products or services. As an affiliate marketer, you provide a unique link or code to your affiliate partners, and they use it to promote your products or services to their audience. Whenever a customer makes a purchase through one of your affiliate partner's links, you pay them a commission for the sale.

The power of affiliate marketing lies in its ability to reach a larger audience than you could on your own. By partnering with other businesses and influencers, you can tap into their audience and reach new customers who may not have heard of your brand before. In addition, affiliate marketing can help you increase your sales and revenue without the need for large advertising budgets.

To get started with affiliate marketing, you need to identify your target audience and find businesses and influencers that cater to that audience. Once you have identified your affiliates, you need to create a strong affiliate program that incentivizes them to promote your products or services. This can include offering a commission on sales, providing exclusive discounts and promotions, or offering bonuses for reaching specific performance milestones.

To maximize the success of your affiliate marketing program, it is important to continuously monitor and optimize your campaigns. You should track your affiliate sales, analyze your conversion rates, and make changes to your affiliate program as needed. By regularly monitoring your program, you can identify which affiliates are driving the most sales and adjust your incentives to encourage them to promote your products even more.

In conclusion, affiliate marketing is a powerful tool for businesses looking to reach new audiences, increase sales, and grow their business. By partnering with other businesses and influencers, you can leverage their audience to reach new customers and achieve your marketing goals.

Public Relations (PR) - Discuss how to build a positive image and reputation for your business through media coverage and public relations efforts.

Public Relations, often abbreviated as PR, is a crucial aspect of marketing that focuses on building and maintaining a positive image and reputation for a business. It is the process of managing and shaping the perception of an organization, product, or service through various communication channels such as the media, social media, and public speaking events.

The main goal of PR is to create and maintain a positive image and reputation for a business that can attract customers and stakeholders, and also increase brand loyalty. By creating and maintaining a positive image, businesses can establish trust and credibility with their target audience, and create a strong reputation in the market.

There are several key components of a successful PR strategy:

Media Relations: Building and maintaining relationships with journalists, bloggers, and other members of the media to secure positive media coverage. This can include writing and distributing press releases, responding to media inquiries, and organizing media events.

Crisis Management: Developing and implementing strategies for handling negative publicity, crisis communication, and damage control.

Content Creation: Developing and distributing content, such as press releases, news articles, blog posts, and social media posts, that promotes the business and its products or services.

Event Planning: Planning and executing events such as product launches, press conferences, and speaking engagements, that can generate positive media coverage and build relationships with key stakeholders.

Influencer Relations: Building relationships with influencers and key opinion leaders in the industry to increase brand visibility and reach new audiences.

To build a successful PR strategy, businesses should start by conducting a thorough analysis of their target audience, industry, and competitors. This will help identify the most effective communication channels and tactics to reach the target audience and achieve the desired results.

By implementing a comprehensive PR strategy, businesses can build a positive image and reputation, increase brand visibility and reach, and establish trust and credibility with their target audience. This can lead to increased sales and a stronger competitive position in the market.

As we come to the end of this comprehensive guide on Game Changer Sales Solutions, we hope you have gained valuable insights and practical tips on how to improve your sales and marketing efforts. From leveraging the power of social media, to creating engaging content, to optimizing your website for conversions, we have covered a wide range of strategies and tactics that can help you drive growth for your business.

We understand that sales and marketing can be a complex and constantly evolving field, but with the right tools and approach, you can achieve remarkable results. The key is to be intentional and consistent in your efforts, and to continually measure and analyze your results so you can make informed decisions and refine your approach.

So, take the knowledge and tips you have learned from this guide and start putting them into action. Remember, success in sales and marketing is a journey, not a destination. Keep learning, experimenting, and refining your strategies and you will find the results you are looking for.

In conclusion, we would like to thank you for taking the time to read this guide, and we wish you all the best in your sales and marketing efforts. May your business grow and flourish, and may your efforts pay off in the form of increased sales, happy customers, and a thriving business.

CHAPTER 25: INTEGRATED MARKETING: THE POWER OF COMBINING CHANNELS FOR OPTIMAL RESULTS

In today's highly competitive business world, it's important to have a comprehensive sales strategy in place to achieve success. In this chapter, we will cover a wide range of topics that are essential for maximizing sales and reaching your target audience. From social media marketing to affiliate marketing and public relations, each topic will provide valuable insights and actionable tips to help you reach your sales goals. By the end of this chapter, you will have a clear understanding of the various components of a successful sales solution and how to effectively implement them in your own business.

Email automation -

Email automation has revolutionized the way businesses approach email marketing. With the help of email marketing software, businesses can now automate repetitive tasks, freeing up time and resources that can be spent on more critical areas of their business. More importantly, email automation enables businesses to create targeted campaigns that can be triggered by specific actions or events. This results in more personalized and effective email marketing, which can increase open rates, click-through rates, conversions, and overall customer engagement.

What is Email Automation?

Email automation refers to the process of using email marketing software to automate repetitive tasks and create targeted campaigns. The software helps to streamline the email marketing process by automating tasks such as sending welcome emails to new subscribers, sending abandoned cart reminders, and sending promotional emails. The software can also be programmed to trigger specific campaigns based on specific actions or events, such as a customer making a purchase or signing up for a newsletter.

Benefits of Email Automation

There are several benefits of email automation, including:

Increased Personalization: Email automation enables businesses to send highly personalized emails based on subscriber behavior, preferences, and interests. This results in higher open rates and click-through rates as subscribers feel that the emails are more relevant to them.

Improved Efficiency: By automating repetitive tasks, businesses can save time and resources that can be spent on other critical areas of their business. The software also eliminates the need for manual emailing, which reduces the chances of human error.

Increased Engagement: Automated emails are triggered by specific actions or events, ensuring that they are delivered at the right time, to the right person, and with the right message. This results in higher engagement and better conversion rates.

Better Data Collection and Analysis: Email automation software provides valuable insights into subscriber behavior and preferences, which can be used to improve future email marketing campaigns. The software also tracks important metrics such as open rates, click-through rates, and conversions, allowing businesses to measure the success of their campaigns.

Types of Email Automation Campaigns

There are several types of email automation campaigns, including:

Welcome Emails: Welcome emails are sent to new subscribers to introduce the brand and thank them for signing up. They often include a special offer or discount to encourage subscribers to make a purchase.

Abandoned Cart Reminders: Abandoned cart reminders are sent to customers who have left items in their shopping cart without making a purchase. The emails serve as a gentle reminder and often include a special offer to encourage customers to complete their purchase.

Promotional Emails: Promotional emails are sent to subscribers to promote products or services. They can be triggered by specific events, such as a sale or special offer, or they can be sent on a regular basis to keep subscribers engaged with the brand.

Re-engagement Emails: Re-engagement emails are sent to subscribers who have become inactive, with the aim of rekindling their interest in the brand. The emails may include a special offer or an invitation to participate in a survey or contest.

Post-Purchase Emails: Post-purchase emails are sent to customers after they have made a purchase. They may include a thank you message, a request for feedback, or a special offer to encourage repeat business.

Conclusion

In conclusion, email automation is a powerful tool for businesses looking to optimize their email marketing efforts. By automating repetitive tasks and creating targeted campaigns, businesses can save time and resources while still delivering effective and personalized messages to their customers. Whether it's welcome messages, abandoned cart reminders, or post-purchase follow-ups, email automation can help businesses create a more streamlined and efficient email marketing process. To get started with email automation, it is important to choose the right email marketing software, define your target audience and goals, and plan out your campaigns.

With the right strategy in place, email automation can be a game changer for your business, helping you build stronger relationships with customers, increase engagement, and drive more sales.

Interactive Content -

Interactive content is a type of digital marketing that involves creating engaging and educational experiences for your target audience. Whether it's through quizzes, polls, surveys, or other forms of interactive content, the goal is to get your audience involved and interacting with your brand in a meaningful way.

The benefits of using interactive content in your marketing strategy are numerous. For one, it can help you build a deeper connection with your audience by providing them with an enjoyable, educational experience. Additionally, interactive content can help increase brand awareness by giving your audience a reason to share your content with their friends and followers. Finally, interactive content can also drive conversions by capturing valuable information about your audience, such as their interests, preferences, and buying behavior.

To get started with interactive content, the first step is to choose a type of content that aligns with your brand's goals and target audience. For example, if you're a retailer looking to increase conversions, you might consider creating a product quiz that helps your audience determine the right product for their needs. Alternatively, if you're a B2B company looking to educate your audience on your industry, you might create a survey or poll that asks your audience questions about a particular topic.

Once you've chosen a type of interactive content, the next step is to create your content. This can involve designing a quiz, poll, or survey, or creating other interactive elements such as graphics, videos, or animations. When designing your content, be sure to keep your audience in mind and make your content as engaging and educational as possible.

Finally, it's important to promote your interactive content and measure its performance. You can do this by sharing your content on social media, embedding it on your website, or including it in your email marketing campaigns. To measure performance, be sure to track metrics such as engagement, completion rate, and conversions, and use this data to continuously improve your interactive content strategy.

In conclusion, interactive content is an effective way to engage and educate your audience, increase brand awareness, and drive conversions. By choosing the right type of content, creating engaging and educational experiences, and promoting and measuring your content's performance, you can achieve success with your interactive content marketing efforts.

Interactive Experiences -

Interactive experiences have become an increasingly popular way for businesses to engage with their customers and stand out in a crowded market. Virtual reality (VR) and augmented reality (AR) are two technologies that are leading the charge in this area, offering customers new and exciting ways to interact with brands.

Virtual reality allows users to fully immerse themselves in a simulated environment, giving them a sense of presence and a feeling of being transported to another world. For businesses, this means creating fully interactive and engaging experiences that can be used to educate, entertain, or promote their products or services.

Augmented reality, on the other hand, enhances the real world by overlaying digital information on the physical environment. This can be used to create unique and interactive experiences that allow users to engage with a brand in a new and innovative way.

One of the biggest benefits of interactive experiences is that they allow businesses to create a deeper level of engagement with their customers. By creating an experience that is not only entertaining but also educational, businesses can increase brand awareness and drive conversions.

In addition to increasing engagement, interactive experiences can also provide valuable insights into customer behavior and preferences. By analyzing user data and feedback, businesses can gain a deeper understanding of what their customers want and need, allowing them to better tailor their products or services to meet these needs.

To succeed with interactive experiences, it is important to have a clear strategy in place. This should involve identifying your target audience, determining what type of experience will best meet their needs, and choosing the right technology to bring your vision to life.

In conclusion, interactive experiences are an exciting and effective way for businesses to engage with their customers and stand out in a crowded market. By creating immersive and interactive experiences that provide value and education, businesses can increase brand awareness and drive conversions, while also gaining valuable insights into customer behavior and preferences.

Virtual Events -

Virtual events have become an increasingly popular way for businesses to connect with their audience and promote their products or services. With the rise of remote work and social distancing, virtual events have proven to be a convenient and effective solution for businesses to reach their target market without the limitations of physical location.

Virtual events can range from webinars, online conferences, and virtual trade shows to virtual product launches and virtual networking events. The main goal of virtual events is to bring people together and provide a platform for engagement and interaction.

Benefits of Virtual Events

Wide reach: Virtual events can be attended by anyone with an internet connection, regardless of their location. This makes it possible for businesses to reach a wider audience, including potential customers from all over the world.

Cost-effective: Virtual events are typically much more cost-effective than traditional in-person events. Businesses can save on travel, lodging, and other related expenses while still providing their audience with a high-quality experience.

Engaging content: Virtual events offer businesses the opportunity to create engaging and interactive content that can help educate and inform their audience. This can include presentations, live Q&A sessions, and virtual tours.

Lead generation: Virtual events provide businesses with an excellent opportunity to generate leads and build relationships with potential customers. Businesses can collect data on attendees and use this information to create targeted marketing campaigns in the future.

Analytics and measurement: Virtual events provide businesses with real-time data and analytics on their audience and the success of their event. This information can be used to improve future events and create more effective marketing strategies.

Tips for Successful Virtual Events

Define your target audience: Determine who you want to reach with your virtual event and tailor your content and marketing efforts to meet their needs and interests.

Create a clear agenda: Clearly define the purpose and goals of your virtual event and provide a clear agenda for attendees. This will help to keep the event focused and on track.

Invest in technology: Ensure that you have the right technology and equipment to create a high-quality virtual event. This can include high-quality cameras, lighting, and sound equipment.

Promote your event: Market your virtual event effectively through a variety of channels, including social media, email marketing, and online ads.

Engage your audience: Encourage audience participation and interaction through live Q&A sessions, surveys, and other interactive elements.

In conclusion, virtual events provide businesses with a cost-effective and efficient way to reach their target market, build relationships, and promote their products or services. By effectively planning, promoting, and executing virtual events, businesses can engage with their audience, generate leads, and drive conversions.

Artificial Intelligence and Machine Learning -

Artificial Intelligence (AI) and Machine Learning (ML) are rapidly transforming the marketing landscape. By leveraging the power of these technologies, businesses can improve their marketing results, better understand their customers, and deliver personalized experiences that drive engagement and sales.

One of the key benefits of AI and ML is the ability to analyze large amounts of data to identify patterns and make predictions. This can be used to optimize marketing campaigns, target the right audience with the right message, and improve the overall customer experience.

Another major advantage of AI and ML is their ability to automate repetitive tasks, freeing up time and resources that can be better spent on higher-value activities. For example, AI-powered chatbots can handle customer service inquiries, freeing up customer service teams to focus on more complex issues.

There are many different applications of AI and ML in marketing, including:

Personalization: AI and ML can be used to personalize customer experiences based on their preferences, behaviors, and interactions with your brand. This can be accomplished through targeted marketing campaigns, website customization, and chatbots that offer personalized recommendations.

Predictive modeling: AI and ML can be used to analyze customer data to predict future behaviors, such as likelihood to purchase or churn. This can be used to proactively reach out to at-risk customers, improve customer retention, and optimize marketing campaigns.

Customer service automation: AI-powered chatbots can be used to handle routine customer service inquiries, freeing up customer service teams to focus on more complex issues.

Data analysis: AI and ML can be used to analyze customer data to identify trends and patterns, allowing you to gain deeper insights into customer behaviors and preferences.

By implementing AI and ML in your marketing efforts, you can achieve greater efficiency, improved results, and a better overall customer experience. Whether you're a large enterprise or a small business, AI and ML offer a range of benefits that can help you achieve your marketing goals and grow your business.

Account-Based Marketing (ABM) -

Account-Based Marketing, or ABM, is a strategic approach that focuses on identifying, engaging and nurturing specific accounts or organizations rather than broad target audiences. Unlike traditional marketing approaches that cast a wide net and hope to reach as many people as possible, ABM is designed to be highly targeted and personalized, ensuring that your marketing efforts are directed at the most valuable prospects.

ABM is particularly effective for B2B companies that sell complex products or services to other businesses. It allows you to focus your marketing efforts on high-value accounts that are most likely to generate significant revenue for your business. By using ABM, you can increase the efficiency and impact of your marketing programs, and improve your return on investment (ROI).

In this chapter, we will discuss the basics of ABM, including its benefits and how it differs from other marketing approaches. We will also discuss the key elements of a successful ABM program, including account identification, account profiling, account segmentation, and account engagement.

To get started with ABM, it's important to understand your target accounts and the challenges they face. This requires deep research and analysis, as well as a thorough understanding of your target market and industry. Once you have identified your target accounts, you can then build a tailored ABM program that meets their specific needs and challenges.

An effective ABM program will include a variety of marketing tactics, such as targeted email campaigns, personalized website experiences, and tailored events and webinars. It's important to measure the success of your ABM program and adjust your tactics as needed to ensure that you are achieving your desired results.

In conclusion, ABM is a strategic approach to marketing that allows businesses to focus their efforts on the most valuable prospects and drive results. By understanding your target accounts and tailoring your marketing efforts to meet their specific needs and challenges, you can improve the efficiency and impact of your marketing programs and generate significant ROI for your business.

Voice Search Optimization -

In recent years, the rise of voice-activated devices such as Amazon Echo and Google Home has changed the way people interact with technology. With the growing popularity of these devices, it is becoming increasingly important for businesses to optimize their websites and content for voice search. This requires a different approach to traditional search engine optimization, as voice search queries tend to be longer and more conversational.

Voice search optimization involves making your website and content accessible and easily understandable by voice-activated devices. This means focusing on natural language keywords and making sure your content is organized in a clear, concise manner that is easy for users to understand.

One important aspect of voice search optimization is ensuring your website is mobile-friendly. As more and more people use voice-activated devices on the go, it is crucial that your website is optimized for mobile devices and loads quickly on a variety of devices and internet speeds.

Additionally, including structured data on your website can help improve your voice search results. Structured data is information about your website that is coded in a way that is easily understood by search engines. This information can help voice-activated devices understand the context of your website and return more accurate results to users.

Another important aspect of voice search optimization is making sure your website is secure. This is because voice-activated devices typically prioritize secure websites in their search results. This can be accomplished by installing an SSL certificate on your website, which encrypts sensitive information and helps to protect users' privacy.

Finally, it is important to regularly track and monitor your voice search performance to see what is working and what is not. You can use tools such as Google Search Console and Google Analytics to see how your website is performing in voice search results, and make adjustments as needed to improve your results.

In conclusion, voice search optimization is an increasingly important aspect of digital marketing. By focusing on mobile-friendliness, structured data, website security, and ongoing performance tracking, businesses can improve their visibility and reach in voice search results, helping to drive more traffic, leads, and sales.

CHAPTER 26 VIRAL MARKETING BEYOND THE DIGITAL WORLD: SECRETS TO SPARK WORD-OF-MOUTH AND DRIVE GROWTH

In the age of digital technology, businesses are often focused on online marketing strategies to reach their target audience. While online marketing is an important aspect of modern-day marketing, there are still plenty of opportunities for businesses to make an impact through non-digital methods. This chapter will explore various non-digital viral marketing secrets that businesses can use to boost their marketing efforts and reach a wider audience. From word-of-mouth marketing to experiential events, we will cover a range of strategies and techniques that can help businesses create a buzz and get people talking about their brand.

Leverage word-of-mouth:

Word-of-mouth marketing has been a trusted and effective marketing tool for centuries, and it continues to be an important part of any marketing strategy. This form of marketing is based on the idea that people trust the recommendations of their friends, family, and colleagues more than they trust advertisements. By leveraging the power of word-of-mouth, businesses can reach new audiences and increase their sales.

In this chapter, we will explore the various strategies and tactics that businesses can use to encourage their customers to spread the word about their products or services. We will also discuss the importance of incentivizing word-of-mouth marketing through referral bonuses and campaigns.

The Power of Word-of-Mouth Marketing

Word-of-mouth marketing is one of the most powerful marketing tools available. According to a Nielson study, 92% of consumers trust recommendations from friends and family more than any other form of advertising. This means that when someone recommends a product or service to their friends and family, there is a high likelihood that they will trust the recommendation and consider making a purchase.

Encouraging Word-of-Mouth Marketing
There are several ways businesses can encourage their customers to spread the word about their products or services. One of the most effective ways is to deliver exceptional customer service. When customers are happy with the service they receive, they are more likely to recommend the business to their friends and family.

Another way to encourage word-of-mouth marketing is to offer referral bonuses or run referral campaigns. This can be as simple as offering a discount or a free product to customers who refer a certain number of people to the business. These incentives can be an effective way to encourage customers to spread the word and bring new customers to the business.

The Benefits of Word-of-Mouth Marketing
In addition to reaching new audiences, word-of-mouth marketing can also have several other benefits for businesses. For example, it can help build brand awareness and increase brand loyalty. When customers are satisfied with the products or services they receive, they are more likely to become repeat customers and promote the business to others.

Furthermore, word-of-mouth marketing can be cost-effective, as it doesn't require any advertising budget. This makes it an attractive option for small businesses and startups.

Conclusion:

In conclusion, word-of-mouth marketing is an important part of any marketing strategy. By delivering exceptional customer service and incentivizing word-of-mouth through referral bonuses and campaigns, businesses can encourage their customers to spread the word about their products or services. This can help reach new audiences, build brand awareness, and increase sales. Leveraging the power of word-of-mouth marketing can be a game changer for businesses of all sizes.

Use influencer marketing:

Influencer marketing is a powerful tool that can help businesses reach new audiences, increase brand awareness, and build their reputation. Influencer marketing involves partnering with individuals who have a significant following and influence over their followers. These influencers can promote your products or services to their audience, helping you reach potential customers you may not have been able to reach on your own.

The success of an influencer marketing campaign is largely dependent on choosing the right influencer to partner with. The influencer should align with your brand values, have a engaged following, and reach your target audience. It is also important to be transparent about the relationship between your brand and the influencer, as authenticity is key to building trust with your audience.

When done correctly, influencer marketing can be an effective way to drive sales, increase brand loyalty, and build a positive reputation. Whether through sponsored posts, product reviews, or influencer events, there are many ways to work with influencers to achieve your marketing goals.

In this chapter, we will explore the benefits of influencer marketing and the steps you can take to identify the right influencer for your brand. We will also discuss the different types of influencer partnerships, and how to measure the success of your influencer marketing campaign. Whether you are just starting out with influencer marketing or are looking to take your efforts to the next level, this chapter will provide you with the insights and strategies you need to succeed.

Influencer marketing has become one of the most effective and popular marketing strategies in recent years. By partnering with influential individuals in your industry or niche, you can reach new audiences and build brand awareness in a way that is authentic and engaging. Influencer marketing is particularly effective because it leverages the credibility and trust that influencers have built with their followers, making it more likely that their followers will take action based on their recommendations.

To get started with influencer marketing, the first step is to identify the right influencer for your brand. To do this, you should look for influencers who have a large and engaged following, and who align with your brand values and target audience. You can use tools such as social media analytics and influencer marketing platforms to research and compare potential influencers.

Once you have identified your ideal influencer, the next step is to reach out to them and discuss the potential for a partnership. There are several different types of influencer partnerships, including product reviews, sponsored posts, and brand ambassadorships. The type of partnership you choose will depend on your goals, budget, and the influencer's area of expertise.

To measure the success of your influencer marketing campaign, it is important to track key metrics such as engagement rates, website traffic, and sales. You can use tools such as Google Analytics and social media analytics to track these metrics, and adjust your strategy accordingly.

Overall, influencer marketing can be a powerful and effective way to reach new audiences and build your brand. By partnering with the right influencer and using data-driven strategies, you can maximize the impact of your influencer marketing efforts and achieve your marketing goals.

Here are some websites that can help you find influencers for your brand:

Upfluence
AspireIQ
Influencer.co
HypeAuditor
Tribe Dynamics
Grin
Buzzsumo
Fohr
Klear
Afluencer
NeoReach

Each of these platforms has its own unique features and pricing models, so it's worth exploring them to find the one that best suits your needs and budget. Additionally, social media platforms such as Instagram, TikTok, and YouTube also offer built-in influencer search tools that you can use to find relevant influencers in your niche.

Organize events:

Hosting events can be a powerful marketing tool for businesses of all sizes. Whether you are launching a new product, participating in a trade show, or hosting a conference, events can help you reach new audiences, build relationships, and generate interest in your brand.

In this chapter, we will explore the benefits of event marketing and the different types of events you can organize. We will also discuss how to plan and execute a successful event, including how to choose the right venue, create an engaging program, and promote your event to your target audience.

By the end of this chapter, you will have a better understanding of the role events can play in your marketing strategy, and the steps you can take to make your next event a success.

Whether you are looking to launch a new product, build brand awareness, or engage with your customers, events can help you achieve your marketing goals. By creating a memorable and engaging experience, you can leave a lasting impression on your audience and generate interest in your business for years to come.

Leverage partnerships:

Partnerships can be a powerful tool for businesses looking to expand their reach and build their brand. By aligning with other businesses, organizations, or media outlets, you can leverage their resources and expertise to reach new audiences and tap into their existing networks. In this chapter, we will explore the benefits of partnerships, how to identify potential partners, and the steps you can take to build successful partnerships. Whether you are looking to drive sales, increase brand awareness, or simply expand your network, this chapter will provide you with the insights and strategies you need to succeed.

Benefits of Partnerships:
Partnerships can offer a range of benefits to businesses of all sizes. Some of the key benefits include:

Increased reach: By partnering with other businesses, organizations, or media outlets, you can access new audiences and tap into their existing networks. This can help you expand your reach and increase brand awareness.
Cost savings: Partnerships can help you pool resources and reduce costs, making it easier and more cost-effective to achieve your goals.
Shared expertise: By working with partners, you can leverage their expertise and knowledge to improve your business.

Increased credibility: Partnerships can help build your credibility and reputation, especially if you partner with well-established organizations or media outlets.

Identifying Potential Partners:

The first step in building successful partnerships is to identify potential partners. To do this, you should consider the following factors:

Compatibility: Look for partners that share your values, goals, and vision. This will ensure that your partnership is built on a strong foundation and is more likely to succeed.

Reach: Consider partners that have a large following or a strong network. This will help you reach new audiences and expand your reach.

Expertise: Look for partners that have expertise in areas that can benefit your business. For example, if you are looking to expand your marketing efforts, you may want to partner with a marketing agency.

Building Successful Partnerships:

Once you have identified potential partners, the next step is to build successful partnerships. To do this, you should consider the following steps:

Define your goals: Clearly define your goals for the partnership, including what you hope to achieve and how you will measure success.

Develop a plan: Create a plan for how you will work with your partner, including how you will communicate, who will be responsible for what, and how you will handle conflicts.

Communicate regularly: Regular communication is key to building successful partnerships. Make sure to keep your partner informed and up-to-date on your progress and any changes to your plans.

Measure success: Regularly measure the success of your partnership and adjust your strategy as needed. This will help you ensure that your partnership is delivering the results you need to grow your business.

Conclusion:

Leveraging partnerships can be a powerful tool for businesses looking to expand their reach and build their brand. By aligning with other businesses, organizations, or media outlets, you can access new audiences and tap into their existing networks, as well as pool resources and reduce costs. To be successful, it is important to identify the right partners, define your goals, develop a plan, communicate regularly, and measure success. With the right approach, partnerships can help you achieve your goals and drive business growth.

Offer free samples or trials:

One of the most effective marketing strategies for any business is to offer customers a free taste of what you have to offer. By providing free samples or trials, you can create interest and generate buzz about your products or services. This not only attracts new customers, but it can also help build loyalty among your existing customers.

Offering free samples or trials can be a low-risk and low-cost way to introduce people to your business and help them experience the benefits of your products or services first-hand. This can be especially effective for businesses that are selling something that is difficult to explain, or for those that are selling products or services that are new to the market.

To be successful, it is important to have a clear strategy in place when offering free samples or trials. This can include setting goals, determining your target audience, and figuring out the best way to promote your offer. You should also consider the cost of providing the samples or trials, and how you will measure the success of your campaign.

When done right, offering free samples or trials can be a powerful tool for building brand awareness, generating leads, and increasing sales. Whether you are a start-up or an established business, this marketing strategy can help you reach new customers and take your business to the next level.

Create engaging content:

One of the most effective marketing strategies for any business is to offer customers a free taste of what you have to offer. By providing free samples or trials, you can create interest and generate buzz about your products or services. This not only attracts new customers, but it can also help build loyalty among your existing customers.

Offering free samples or trials can be a low-risk and low-cost way to introduce people to your business and help them experience the benefits of your products or services first-hand. This can be especially effective for businesses that are selling something that is difficult to explain, or for those that are selling products or services that are new to the market.

To be successful, it is important to have a clear strategy in place when offering free samples or trials. This can include setting goals, determining your target audience, and figuring out the best way to promote your offer. You should also consider the cost of providing the samples or trials, and how you will measure the success of your campaign.

When done right, offering free samples or trials can be a powerful tool for building brand awareness, generating leads, and increasing sales. Whether you are a start-up or an established business, this marketing strategy can help you reach new customers and take your business to the next level.

Engage with your audience:

In today's digital age, customer engagement has become an important aspect of any successful marketing strategy. Engaging with your audience helps build relationships and increase brand loyalty, which can lead to repeat business and positive word-of-mouth recommendations. In this chapter, we will discuss the various ways you can engage with your audience and how this can benefit your business.

Responding to Customer Feedback:

One of the most effective ways to engage with your audience is by responding to customer feedback. Whether it is a positive review or a negative complaint, responding to customer feedback shows that you value their opinions and are committed to improving your products or services. You can respond to feedback through various channels such as email, social media, or online reviews.

Interacting on Social Media:

Social media is an important platform for engaging with your audience. You can interact with customers by responding to comments, posting updates, and running contests or promotions. Social media also provides an opportunity to share behind-the-scenes content, showcase your brand's personality, and share customer stories.

Participating in Online Communities:

Participating in online communities related to your industry or niche can help you engage with potential customers and build relationships. You can participate in these communities by sharing your expertise, answering questions, and engaging in discussions. By participating in online communities, you can establish yourself as a thought leader and build credibility for your business.

Conclusion:

In conclusion, engaging with your audience is a critical component of any successful marketing strategy. By responding to customer feedback, interacting on social media, and participating in online communities, you can build relationships, increase brand loyalty, and ultimately drive growth for your business. Whether you are just starting out or looking to improve your engagement efforts, implementing these strategies can help you achieve your marketing goals.

Create shareable experiences:

In today's fast-paced digital world, word-of-mouth marketing has become one of the most effective and powerful forms of marketing. By creating shareable experiences, you can tap into the natural human desire to share information and opinions with others, and harness the power of word-of-mouth to drive awareness and interest in your brand.

Benefits of Creating Shareable Experiences:

There are many benefits to creating shareable experiences for your customers. For one, it can help to build brand loyalty and strengthen relationships with your customers. By providing them with an enjoyable, memorable experience, you encourage them to share their positive experiences with others, which in turn, can help to drive more business and build your reputation.

In addition, creating shareable experiences can help to generate positive word-of-mouth, which is often more trusted and persuasive than traditional advertising. This is because people are more likely to trust recommendations from friends, family, and peers than from anonymous advertisements or advertisements from unfamiliar sources.

Designing Shareable Experiences:

To create shareable experiences, you must first understand what motivates people to share their experiences with others. This could be because they have had a particularly enjoyable experience, or because they have discovered something new and exciting. Whatever the reason, it is important to design your products, services, or customer experiences in a way that encourages sharing.

One way to do this is to create memorable experiences. For example, you could host a special event or create a unique product that customers will want to tell others about. Another way is to create experiences that are highly personalized and relevant to each customer, such as customized product recommendations based on their interests and preferences.

Measuring Success:

To measure the success of your efforts to create shareable experiences, it is important to track key metrics such as the number of customer referrals, the number of social media shares and mentions, and the number of positive reviews and testimonials.

Conclusion:

By creating shareable experiences, you can tap into the power of word-of-mouth marketing and drive interest in your brand. Whether it is through hosting special events, providing personalized experiences, or designing products that encourage sharing, the key is to understand what motivates customers to share their experiences and then create experiences that meet those motivations. With the right approach and a focus on measurement, you can successfully leverage the power of word-of-mouth marketing to grow your business.

By incorporating these viral marketing secrets into your overall marketing strategy, you can increase the chances of your marketing efforts going viral and reaching a wider audience.

RESOURCES AVAILABLE TO HELP MARKET A BUSINESS, INCLUDING:

Social media platforms: Utilize platforms like Facebook, Twitter, and Instagram to reach customers, build relationships, and share content.

Marketing and advertising tools: Use tools like Google Ads, Bing Ads, and Facebook Ads to run targeted ad campaigns and drive traffic to your website.

Content marketing: Use blogs, videos, and other forms of content to educate and engage customers and establish your brand as an authority in your industry.

Influencer marketing: Partner with influencers in your industry or niche to reach new audiences and build your brand's reputation.

Email marketing: Use email marketing software to automate repetitive tasks and create targeted campaigns that can be triggered by specific actions or events.

Trade shows and events: Attend trade shows and other events to network with potential customers, partners, and other businesses in your industry.

PR and media relations: Work with journalists and other members of the media to secure media coverage and build your brand's reputation.

Industry associations and trade organizations: Join industry associations and trade organizations to network with other businesses and stay up-to-date on industry trends and best practices.

Marketing and branding agencies: Hire a marketing or branding agency to help develop and execute a comprehensive marketing strategy for your business.

Online courses and workshops: Take online courses or attend workshops to learn new marketing skills and stay up-to-date on industry trends and best practices.

Here are some highly recommended books for marketing:

- "Contagious: How to Build Word of Mouth in the Digital Age" by Jonah Berger
- "Influence: The Psychology of Persuasion" by Robert Cialdini
- "Made to Stick: Why Some Ideas Survive and Others Die" by Chip Heath and Dan Heath
- "The Lean Startup: How Today's Entrepreneurs Use Continuous Innovation to Create Radically Successful Businesses" by Eric Ries
- "Start with Why: How Great Leaders Inspire Everyone to Take Action" by Simon Sinek
- "Marketing Management" by Philip Kotler
- "Duct Tape Marketing: The World's Most Practical Small Business Marketing Guide" by John Jantsch
- "The Challenger Customer: Selling to the Hidden Influencer Who Can Multiply Your Results" by Brent Adamson and Matthew Dixon
- "Building a StoryBrand: Clarify Your Message So Customers Will Listen" by Donald Miller
- "Hooked: How to Build Habit-Forming Products" by Nir Eyal.

These books offer insights, strategies, and case studies to help you understand the principles of marketing and how to effectively promote your business.

Here are some websites that can help with marketing:

- Hubspot: A leading inbound marketing and sales platform that offers tools and resources for content creation, email marketing, social media, and more.

- Moz: A platform that provides SEO tools and resources, including keyword research, site audit, and link building tools.

- Buffer: A social media management tool that allows you to schedule and publish posts, track analytics, and collaborate with team members.

- SEMrush: A platform that offers a range of digital marketing tools, including keyword research, site audit, and competitive analysis.

- Canva: A graphic design platform that allows you to create beautiful graphics and visual content for your marketing efforts.

- Hootsuite: A social media management tool that allows you to schedule and publish posts, track analytics, and collaborate with team members.

- CoSchedule: A content marketing platform that offers tools for organizing and executing your content marketing strategy, including editorial calendars and content optimization.

- Mailchimp: An email marketing platform that offers templates, automation, and analytics to help you send effective and targeted email campaigns.

- Google Analytics: A free analytics platform that provides insights into your website traffic, audience, and marketing performance.

These are just a few of the many websites and tools available to help with marketing. It's important to find the right resources for your specific business needs and goals.

In conclusion, marketing is a crucial component of any successful business. Whether you are just starting out or looking to take your marketing efforts to the next level, there are a variety of strategies and tactics to consider. From developing a strong brand image and building a reputation through public relations, to leveraging interactive content and virtual events, to implementing the latest technologies such as artificial intelligence and machine learning, the opportunities for marketing your business are endless.

In this book, we have explored the many facets of modern marketing and offered insights and strategies to help you succeed. We have covered topics such as email automation, account-based marketing, voice search optimization, influencer marketing, event planning, partnerships, free samples and trials, audience engagement, and shareable experiences.

At the end of the day, the key to successful marketing is to understand your target audience and deliver value to them in a way that is meaningful and relevant. By following the strategies outlined in this book, you can create a strong marketing plan and take your business to the next level.

Remember, marketing is not a one-time effort, but rather a continuous process of testing, learning, and refining. Stay open to new ideas and opportunities, and be willing to pivot and adjust your strategies as needed. With the right approach, you can create a successful marketing campaign that generates leads, builds your brand, and drives growth for your business.

www.ingramcontent.com/pod-product-compliance
Lightning Source LLC
Chambersburg PA
CBHW040927210326
41597CB00030B/5201